Always BEING READY

McDougal & Associates

Servants of Christ and Stewards of the
Mysteries of God

Always

Being

Ready

Keys to a Closer Walk with Your Creator

Daniel Roberts

ALWAYS BEING READY

Published by:

McDougal & Associates
18896 Greenwell Springs RD
Greenwell Springs, LA 70739
www.thepublishedword.com

McDougal & Associates is dedicated to the spreading of the Gospel of Jesus Christ to as many people as possible in the shortest time possible.

ISBN 978-1-934769-25-6

Printed in the United States of America
For Worldwide Distribution

CONTENTS

FOREWORD

I have known Daniel Roberts now for more than thirty years, and we have worked together for about twenty of those years in city and state prison ministries for the Institutional Crusaders for Christ and also conducted street evangelism and ministered in nursing homes together. For all of those years, I can say that Danny has been a wonderful man of God.

I was blessed to read the manuscript for his new book, *Always Being Ready,* before it went to press, and I find it to be a must read. I know that he has not written the book to impress anyone, and yet I am certainly impressed with it. The manner in which he has articulated his thoughts is praiseworthy.

Many of the important themes he expounds on, especially that of repentance and forgiveness, are warmly welcomed by me. Without these, he shows us, life is a waste of time. We cannot just say that we are Christians and hope it to be so.

I can testify from personal experience that what we write has the power to change lives, and so I say to my brother in Christ, Daniel Roberts, in the words of the Scriptures, *"Therefore, my beloved brethren, be ye stedfast, unmoveable, always abounding in the work of the Lord, forasmuch as ye know that your labour is not in vain in the Lord"* (1 Corinthians 15:58). Keep on keeping on, Brother. This book is a blessing, for you have written from your heart. May God bless you.

Antonio Sealy
Pastor, Rescue Mission Work, Inc.

Just as a man can prevent trouble from thieves by keeping watch for them, so you can avoid trouble by ALWAYS BEING READY for my unannounced return. Matthew 24:43-44, TLB
(Emphasis Mine)

INTRODUCTION

It is one of the tragedies of our time that millions of Christians struggle to maintain a closer relationship with their Creator. Clearly this is not the will of a loving heavenly Father. As His beloved children, we need to know that He is with us daily, and we need to know that we are on good enough terms with Him that when we call upon Him for help in whatever situation, He will answer us.

Nothing could be more important in the twenty-first century, for without the Lord's help, we wouldn't be able to make it through the tragedies and trials that come our way. This is the reason the enemy of our souls is delighted when there arises any obstacle whatsoever to our relationship with God.

And such obstacles do arise. We are human, so we err, and when we do, we often disappoint and sadden the heart of God. We make wrong decisions and have to suffer the consequences. We struggle constantly with our flesh, which is forever wanting to do things that are not pleasing to the Father. We get caught up in the spirit of the times, are influenced by the voices of the crowd around us, and suddenly we find ourselves alienated from God.

The problem is that we don't know what to do when this happens. We know that God is good, but we also know that He is holy, and we have disobeyed Him. To make matters worse, the enemy constantly torments us with these facts and tells us that God is so angry with us that He will never forgive what we have done. So, instead of turning quickly to God and seeking His help in the situation, we allow the enemy to cause us to draw back from our Creator because of shame, and we do nothing to resolve our guilt and pain. As a consequence, things only get worse.

What can we do when we have failed morally or followed the flesh or listened to the twenty-first century crowd, and, as a result, we know that God is not pleased with us? The good news is that there is definitely hope for anyone in this situation. The Bible has clear answers for us, and it shows us that God is more eager to see a restoration of our relationship with Him than we are. If you currently find yourself in spiritual distress because of failure of any kind, *Always Being Ready* will reveal to you the *Keys To a Closer Walk with Your Creator.* Your loving heavenly Father is ready to forgive you and pull you back into His outstretched arms. There is just one simple thing you must do. Repent and seek His forgiveness. He is, even now, waiting to hear your prayer.

Daniel Roberts
Springfield Gardens, New York

PART I

READY FOR WHAT?

CHAPTER 1

READY FOR WHATEVER COMES

Behold, I shew you a mystery; We shall not all sleep,
but we shall all be changed.   1 Corinthians 15:51

What is it that we all need to be ready for? Well, for starters, we need to be ready for whatever each new day brings. We have no way of predicting just what any one of us might face today or tomorrow, but if we are ready (meaning if we know the Lord and are walking in fellowship with Him), it doesn't matter what may come our way. If He is with us, we can deal with life as it comes.

WHAT MAY COME

What comes our way may not be evil or difficult. Instead, it may be a wonderful opportunity or an open door of some kind. When such opportunities arise, however, we must be ready for them, or they will pass us by.

Premature death, either by accident or sickness, is one of the very real things we must all be ready for. No man or woman (or boy or girl) is given a guarantee of living another day. Although the average lifespan is growing (depending on where you live and how much you had to eat growing up), young people die every day from sudden heart attacks or strokes or from severe diabetes, cancer or other physical afflictions. Even children die prematurely, so what guarantee do we have as adults?

Think of how many thousands of people die every year on our highways, and yet all of us need to travel to our jobs, to church, to the market or to other places. As a result, we have to take the chance of being killed in order to get where we want to go on any given day. The important thing is to be ready when your time comes, however it comes. You may live to be a hundred, or you may die tomorrow. Only God knows for sure.

READY FOR THE RAPTURE

But even if none of these things should ever befall you, you still need to be ready. "Ready for what?" you might ask. Well, Jesus gave us a clear answer. He said:

Just as a man can prevent trouble from thieves by keeping watch for them, so you can avoid trouble by always being ready for my unannounced return.

Matthew 24:43-44, TLB

"Always being ready" for what? *"Always being ready for my unannounced return,"* Jesus said. What does that mean?

When Jesus left the earth to go back to Heaven, after His years of ministry here and after giving Himself as a sacrifice on Calvary for our sins, He sent angels to tell His disciples that He would come back:

Ye men of Galilee, why stand ye gazing up into heaven? this same Jesus, which is taken up from you into heaven, shall so come in like manner as ye have seen him go into heaven.

Acts 1:11

> **When Jesus left the earth to go back to Heaven, ... He sent angels to tell His disciples that He would come back!**

This teaching of Jesus' return to earth was repeated over and over again during the early years of the Church, as the Holy Scriptures were being formed, and generation after generation then grew up believing that He could return

15

at any time. The question uppermost in everyone's mind was always what was the timing of Jesus' return. And there was no answer, for that was one thing Jesus did not teach. The exact timing of His return was to remain a secret. It was to be *"unannounced,"* and for this reason, we must concentrate on *Always Being Ready.*

Actually, Jesus spoke of returning to the earth twice, once to take His people out of the world, and a second time, to set up His Kingdom on the earth. The first visit, when Jesus will appear in the air above us and cause us to rise to be with Him, has come to be called the Rapture, and Paul also described it to the Corinthian believers:

PAUL'S TEACHINGS TO THE CORINTHIANS

But I am telling you this strange and wonderful secret: we shall not all die, but we shall all be given new bodies! It will all happen in a moment, in the twinkling of an eye, when the last trumpet is blown. For there will be a trumpet blast from the sky and all the Christians who have died will suddenly come alive, with new bodies that will never, never die; and then we [Christians] who are still alive shall suddenly have new bodies too. For our earthly bodies, the ones we have now that can die, must be transformed into heavenly bodies that cannot perish but will live forever.

1 Corinthians 15:51-53, TLB

The word *rapture* is not found anywhere in the Bible, and some use that fact to discount this teaching, but because it meant "a catching away," the word came to be used to describe the sudden disappearance, or vanishing, of millions of Christians from the earth. Such a "rapture," also known to many as the Second Coming of Christ, will take place, it seems clear from the Scriptures, before the seven years of the Great Tribulation. Paul was given a revelation of this experience, and he called it as a *"mystery," "a strange and wonderful secret."*

The Rapture of the Church is to be a totally supernatural event. Man will have no control over it, even so much as to know in advance exactly when it will take place. It will be completely controlled by the authority of God and His authority alone. We just need to be ready for it—whenever the Father sees fit for it to happen.

How To Describe Such an Event?

The scriptures I have chosen from God's Holy Word to explain this wonderful event were given by the Holy Spirit to Paul more than two thousand years ago. They will have to speak for me, for I could never find the right words to describe the wonderful comfort and joy of this *"mystery"* that God has promised to His Church. This is what all believers live for, the hope that surely we will see Him one day. Without this hope we are, as Paul noted, *"of all men most miserable"* (1 Corinthians 15:19). This means simply that without the reality of this truth, when we die, it would all be over, and this world would be all there is for mortal man.

But that's not true. Those of us who love the Lord have the promise of a wonderful future with Him.

PAUL'S TEACHINGS TO THE THESSALONIANS

Paul also wrote to the Thessalonians about the Rapture:

> **In order to be ready for this great and mysterious blessing, ... we must repent and be forgiven!**

I can tell you this directly from the Lord: that we who are still living when the Lord returns will not rise to meet him ahead of those who are in their graves. For the Lord himself will come down from heaven with a mighty shout and with the soul-stirring cry of the archangel and the great trumpet-call of God. And the believers who are dead will be the first to rise to meet the Lord. Then we who are still alive and remain on the earth will be caught up with them in the clouds to meet the Lord in the air and remain with him forever. So comfort and encourage each other with this news.

1 Thessalonians 4:15-18, TLB

Surely each of us desires to take part in this supernatural event. So what is required of us? In order to be ready for this great and mysterious blessing, just like being ready for premature death by sickness or accident, or being ready for whatever daily life brings our way, we must repent and be forgiven, and then we must strive to live a righteous life every moment of every day, praying to God always.

A MESSAGE FOR THE FAITHFUL

I have included a message for sinners and backsliders in the final chapter of the book, but the main focus of this message is not for either sinners or backsliders. The purpose of this book is to stir up believers and warn them to be ready. Jesus issued just such a warning to those who loved Him in His day. He said we could *"avoid trouble by always being ready for [His] unannounced return"* (Matthew 24:44).

When will it happen? When will Jesus return for His people? *"In such an hour as ye think not"* (KJV). Therefore, remember to keep your soul and your body under the control of the Holy Spirit, and whenever you fail in any way, run to the Lord quickly and seek His forgiveness.

JOHN'S SEEMINGLY HARSH WORDS

John the Revelator was given these seemingly harsh words:

He that is unjust, let him be unjust still: and he which is filthy, let him be filthy still: and he that is righteous, let him be righteous still: and he that is holy, let him be holy still. And, behold, I come quickly; and my reward is with me, to give every man according as his work shall be. Revelation 22:11-12

But there is nothing harsh about these words. That's just the reality of how it will happen, suddenly and unexpectedly. And when that moment arrives, it will be too late to repent. Now is the time for repentance and forgiveness.

Being prepared for the coming of the Lord (or whatever else tomorrow may bring our way) means living in a state of relationship with Him, and that should be our motivation. Let us not respond in fear to an alarmist endtime message. The glorious hope of hearing the voice of the archangel and the trump of God will be the joy of those who concentrate on *Always Being Ready.*

PART II

THE FORGIVENESS THAT GOD EXTENDS TO US

CHAPTER 2

WHAT IS FORGIVENESS AND HOW IS IT ACQUIRED?

Him hath God exalted with his right hand to be a Prince and a Saviour, for to give repentance to Israel, and forgiveness of sins. And we are his witnesses of these things; and so is also the Holy Ghost, whom God hath given to them that obey him. Acts 5:31-32

There is a very valid reason for repentance, and it is not so that we can grovel in humiliation before God. No! He is not only our Creator; He is also our always loving and kind heavenly Father.

> *Repentance has a redeeming purpose. It is the means of restoring our relationship with our Creator!*

Repentance has a redeeming purpose. It is the means of restoring our relationship with our Creator, and therefore there is no greater act of love than the forgiveness He extends to us when we willingly repent. Just as He extends to us the privilege of repentance, He then also extends to us His forgiveness for our wrongdoing.

REPENTANCE MEANS BEING SORRY

Repentance just means being sorry for what we've done, being sorry enough to confess our wrong to God, and being sorry enough to want not to repeat it. This is the attitude God rewards with forgiveness.

None of us has to pay or could pay for God's forgiveness; He offers it freely. If there was any price for this great demonstration of His love, He paid it all on Calvary, where He made possible your repentance and your forgiveness, taking upon Himself the punishment you deserved. There, on the cross, He paid the debt we owed and took the punishment and sufferings of death for our sins. He died so that we could live.

IT IS GOD WHO GRANTS REPENTANCE AND FORGIVENESS

We see here in our text verse for this chapter that it is God who grants repentance and forgiveness. He offered this great gift to His people Israel, and now, through Christ, He has also extended this gift to every Gentile who will believe. With God, there is never any discrimination. He loves us, no matter who we are or where we're from. He sees us all as sinners and offers us all the same free gift of redemption through the blood of His Son Jesus. All He requires of us is a penitent heart.

Some early Jewish followers of Christ found it difficult to believe that pagan Gentiles could be saved. Returning from his revival among the Gentiles in Caesarea, Peter told them:

Forasmuch then as God gave them the like gift as he did unto us, who believed on the Lord Jesus Christ; what was I, that I could withstand God?   Acts 11:17

Upon hearing this, the Jewish leaders were convinced:

When they heard these things, they held their peace, and glorified God, saying, Then hath God also to the Gentiles granted repentance unto life.   Acts 11:18

Just what is this repentance that God has granted to us? Repentance is a voluntary change of mind, a willingness to turn away from sin. This so pleases the Father that He immediately wipes the record of the sin away and remembers it no more against us.

God grants us the ability and the opportunity to repent, but we have to do the actual repenting. Once we have repented, the wonderful experience of forgiveness is then instantly and automatically granted. This is just another of the gifts from the hand of a loving Father. In this way, God cancels the punishment that was assigned to us for our crime, and we no longer have to pay what was our due. Instead, as a repentant sinner, we are now free from guilt and punishment. How wonderful!

IT'S ALL FREE

One of the most wonderful aspects of God's forgiveness is that it's all free. Nothing that He has for the Church is on sale. Jesus sold nothing, and neither did the apostles, who carried on His work after Him. The Scriptures assure us that He is the same today as He was then:

Jesus Christ the same yesterday, and to-day, and for ever.   Hebrews 13:8

It is important for all Christians to remember this *free* aspect of God's grace and not to attempt to pay for anything that He offers us. This includes physical healing and miracles. Our God is a God of miracles. He did miracles in the days of the apostles:

*And God wrought special miracles by the hands of
Paul: so that from his body were brought unto the sick
handkerchiefs or aprons, and the diseases departed
from them, and the evil spirits went out of them.*

Acts 19:11-12

The Living Bible puts these words into modern Eng-
lish for a better understanding of what actually took
place:

*And God gave Paul the power to do unusual miracles,
so that even when his handkerchiefs or parts of his
clothing were placed upon sick people, they were healed,
and any demons within them came out.*

Acts:19:11-12, TLB

God is still the God of miracles, and He can do the
same *"unusual miracles"* today. We must be careful not to
place our confidence in spiritual gimmickry. Save your
money, and use it for the relief of hunger in poor countries. Never pay for what God offered freely to all who
would trust in Him. If we have trusted in the vain prom-
ises of man, we should repent. Even God's healing virtue
is offered freely.

The Bible charges the more mature believers among
us to pray for the sick, and they are to use anointing oil in
the process, in obedience to the Holy Spirit:

*Is any sick among you? let him call for the elders of
the church; and let them pray over him, anointing him
with oil in the name of the Lord; and the prayer of faith*

shall save the sick, and the Lord shall raise him up; and if he have committed sins, they shall be forgiven him.   James 5:14-15

Is there any way this could be construed as an order for the sick be charged for the oil that is used to anoint them? Absolutely not! Why, then, do some sell oil, as if their particular mix of it had miraculous powers of its own? If the power of the Holy Spirit is not present to heal, you could bathe in gallons of "holy" or "anointed" oil and still receive no healing from it. The healing is not in the oil, but in the Holy Spirit and in obedience to Him.

Compare the wording of these verses from the Living Bible:

Is anyone sick? He should call for the elders of the church and they should pray over him and pour a little oil upon him, calling on the Lord to heal him. And their prayer, if offered in faith, will heal him, for the Lord will make him well; and if his sickness was caused by some sin, the Lord will forgive him.

James 5:14-15, TLB

No matter what translation you read it from, there has never been any indication in the Scriptures that the sick were to pay for the anointing oil used to minister to their needs. As this particular scripture shows, it is not the oil that brings healing, but the prayer of faith in the living God.

And what do the Scriptures mean by *"the prayer of faith"*? It is an unselfish prayer of perseverance offered by a righteous person who has great power with God. Only when the process is carried out under these circumstances will the manifestation of healing come. Still, healing, like forgiveness, is free.

DELIVERING THE SOUL FROM DEATH

There are many teachings that lay the foundations for biblical forgiveness. First and foremost, in the process of forgiveness, God removes our transgressions from us and delivers the soul from eternal death. Only He can do this. What a mighty and sovereign God we serve! No wonder David sang:

> *There are many teachings that lay the foundations for biblical forgiveness!*

Bless the LORD, O my soul, and forget not all his benefits: who forgiveth all thine iniquities; who healeth all thy diseases.

For as the heaven is high above the earth, so great is his mercy toward them that fear him. As far as the east is from the west, so far hath he removed our transgressions from us.   Psalm 103:2-3 and 11-12

Second, forgiveness (a process that includes getting rid of the sin problem and dealing with the sin nature) brings us cleansing and the cancelation of all judgments against us because of sin. Through the power of the blood of Jesus Christ and the Holy Spirit, God delivers our conscience from bondage:

How much more shall the blood of Christ, who through the eternal Spirit offered himself without spot to God, purge your conscience from dead works to serve the living God? Hebrews 9:14

Then there must be forgiveness within the Body of Christ, which is made up of the people of God. We will discuss this important subject in Part III of the book.

UNDER THE WATCHFUL EYE OF THE HOLY SPIRIT

We are constantly under the watchful eye of the Holy Spirit, and He urges us to guard our hearts. When we discover there anything that does not please Him, we have at our disposal the means of wiping the slate clean again. It is God's wonderful gift of repentance and forgiveness.

The prophet Micah declared:

Who is a God like unto thee, that pardoneth iniquity, and passeth by the transgression of the remnant of his heritage? Micah 7:18

In New Testament times, the apostle John wrote to the early Christian Church:

If we confess our sins, he is faithful and just to forgive us our sins, and to cleanse us from all unrighteousness.

*If we say that we have not sinned, we make him a liar,
and his word is not in us.*   1 John 1:9-10

Our God wants us to be happy and rejoicing, but the devil wants us to be miserable, sad and lonely. One thing is certain: there can be no happiness and joy in us while the heart is in bondage and oppression because of unconfessed and unforsaken sins. If we are to remain in right standing with God (what the Bible calls "righteous"), we must learn and put into practice the importance of repentance and receiving God's forgiveness. Only then can we experience the blessing of freedom.

"EXCEPT YE REPENT"

In His day, Jesus taught:

I tell you, Nay: but except ye repent, ye shall all likewise perish.   Luke 13:3

Truth never changes from one generation to another, and forgiveness is one of those established truths. Therefore it will never change over time and eternity. Jesus is *"the truth,"* (John 14:6) and He has declared that unless we *"repent,"* we will *"perish."*

Today, the mere mention of this word *perish* does not set well with our modern generations. Instead, we are being assured that we can improve ourselves, but self-improvement is a doctrine of devils. Man cannot improve himself. A power greater than himself is needed if a man or woman is to effect any kind of improvement in their life. This is a truth that will never ever grow old.

It is the same with forgiveness. These truths are established forever, and they are the foundation upon which the righteousness and justice of God is sealed. Repentance followed by forgiveness is the only acceptable first step toward moral and spiritual transformation. There is no other way. Jesus is *"the way"* (John 14:6) and the only way. It is only in Him that we can become *"a new creature"*:

> *Therefore if any man be in Christ, he is a new creature: old things are passed away; behold, all things are become new.*
>
> 2 Corinthians 5:17

> **These truths are established forever, and they are the foundation upon which the righteousness and justice of God is sealed!**

NO AMOUNT OF MONEY CAN PURCHASE FREEDOM FROM SHAME

No matter how much money a person has kept in the bank, there is never enough to purchase forgiveness when a person is suddenly called to leave this life. No matter how much money a person has given to the church, there is no way that money can atone his or her sins. Still, when men and women commit unspeakable crimes, they insist on hiding their sins and are ashamed to accept God's only means of forgiveness. If Christ died for what we are ashamed of, then all we have to do is humble ourselves and know that He already bore our shame on the cross.

Because of the unspeakable crimes and wickedness people do in this life, they are ashamed to seek forgiveness God's way, so they go about trying to achieve their own righteousness without the benefit of the cross. Some would rather try to deceive others (and they're only deceiving themselves) by offering everything but genuine repentance. Paul wrote:

For by grace are ye saved through faith; and that not of yourselves: it is the gift of God: not of works, lest any man should boast. Ephesians 2:8-9

It is repentance and forgiveness that opens up the way to communication with God and having fellowship with Him through the Holy Spirit. The first prayer He hears from a believer is their prayer of repentance.

It's repentance and forgiveness that brings happiness and rejoicing. This is a manifestation of joy, one of the fruits of the Holy Spirit. Since the offender is now free from all the punishment that is attached to sin, there is reason to rejoice. A happy man or woman is one who has been forgiven and carries no burden of guilt and condemnation on their conscience:

Happy art thou, O Israel: who is like unto thee, O people saved by the LORD, the shield of thy help, and who is the sword of thy excellency! and thine enemies shall be found liars unto thee; and thou shalt tread upon their high places. Deuteronomy 33:29

When Jesus healed those who came to Him, they rejoiced, and there were two reasons for this rejoicing. First, it was because the King of kings had touched them with His supernatural words and hands and healed them. But, secondly, it was also because they had become spiritually whole and could go their way free from guilt and condemnation. Praise God for the free gift of repentance and forgiveness.

NO FORGIVENESS WITHOUT REPENTANCE

Clearly, there can be no forgiveness without repentance. God is holy, He shows no favoritism and neither does He discriminate against anyone—regardless of what people believe or what they may accomplish in life. The Bible shows us that *"all have sinned, and come short of the glory of God"* (Romans 3:23). And God's standard is irreversible and unchangeable. He has said:

That ye may be the children of your Father which is in heaven: for he maketh his sun to rise on the evil and on the good, and he sendeth rain on the just and on the unjust. Matthew 5:45

The sinner may say that he's not responsible for what he does because he was "just wired that way." Well, a man can say whatever he wants to say, but God holds him responsible—regardless of the philosophy he may embrace. God is both Creator and Law Giver, and as such He has the divine right to govern His creation as He sees fit. Man, then, is responsible to obey God's laws, if he wishes to live in this world that he had no part in creating.

When God's laws are disobeyed, creation reacts with justice to display God's displeasure. His wrath and vengeance against the lawbreaker is demonstrated through destructive storms, tornadoes, hurricanes, fires and floods. Sometimes God removes His protective hand, which was once man's defense, and in order to be restored to the position to receive the blessings of God, he must repent and seek forgiveness.

No one who leaves this world the same way he came into it can hope to gain eternal life. Whether we think or believe that we have been "wired" a certain way and cannot change, the God of all holiness and justice warns every man and woman to repent and believe the Gospel. The Rapture is imminent. Don't procrastinate any longer and miss your opportunity to repent and get right with God before it's too late. When we walk in the Spirit we have the guarantee of *Always Being Ready* for the soon return of Jesus Christ.

Chapter 3

The Responsibilities of the Forgiven

And the scribes and Pharisees brought unto him a woman taken in adultery; and when they had set her in the midst, they say unto him, Master, this woman was taken in adultery, in the very act. Now Moses in the law commanded us, that such should be stoned: but what sayest thou?   John 8:3-5

Although forgiveness costs us nothing, there are responsibilities that come with such a great gift, and they are important.

THIS WOMAN DESERVED DEATH

Early in His ministry, Jesus was confronted with this very difficult case of a woman taken in the act of adultery, and it was presented to Him by some very contentious men. He was able to handle both the men and the situation well. The story shows us clearly that God extends forgiveness, even for the serious sin of adultery.

"Stone her to death, because she's an adulterer; we caught her in the very act," were the words of her accusers, but Jesus had other ideas. Instead of killing her, as the Law required, He forgave her and gave her a new life. That's what God's love will do for anyone ready to repent and seek His forgiveness.

It is very clear that the person who sent these men, described here as *"scribes and Pharisees,"* was none other than Satan himself, the accuser, the devil. Jesus, however, was not thrown by their cunning questions. He knew what to answer them. How wonderful!

We, who are filled with the Holy Spirit, must be quick to use the gift of discerning of spirits to know which questions we should answer and what we should say if God gives us the opportunity to address the enemies of His cross. Jesus was ready for this encounter because He had fasted forty days and forty nights alone in the wilderness. There He was tempted by the devil, but He came out of that wilderness experience in victory, and now He could not be deceived by wicked men. Believers, we must pray always to be more like Jesus, so that we can handle anything the devil throws our way.

ONLY TEMPTING HIM

These men were not sincere. They were only *"tempting him"*:

> *This they said, tempting him, that they might have to accuse him. But Jesus stooped down, and with his finger wrote on the ground, as though he heard them not. So when they continued asking him, he lifted up himself, and said unto them, He that is without sin among you, let him first cast a stone at her.*
>
> John 8:6-7

Although forgiveness costs us nothing, there are responsibilities that come with such a great gift, and they are important!

Jesus knew how to frustrate the devil, and every child of God can do the same thing, if he or she will only use wisdom from above. Jesus used the wisest approach. He gave these men no reason to get in a fight over doctrine and the commandments. He allowed them to wear themselves out with their arguments. Then, when He eventually spoke, they were speechless.

When Jesus speaks, devils tremble. They cannot stand against the power of the Word of Almighty God:

And they which heard it, being convicted by their own conscience, went out one by one, beginning at the eldest, even unto the last: and Jesus was left alone, and the woman standing in the midst. When Jesus had lifted up himself, and saw none but the woman, he said unto her, Woman, where are those thine accusers? hath no man condemned thee? She said, No man, Lord. And Jesus said unto her, Neither do I condemn thee; go, and sin no more.　　　　　　　　　　John 8:9-11

ESTABLISHED TRUTHS ABOUT FORGIVENESS

That day, Jesus established some important truths about forgiveness. First, it is extended to all. Second, He calls all who have been forgiven to understand that they now have a responsibility to walk in holiness, righteousness and accountability. Many preach that the Christian life should never become a set of rules: "don't do this and don't do that," but Jesus gave this woman a rule, and the rule showed that there are things a Christian should avoid doing in order to maintain a life of holiness and fellowship with God. *"Go,"* Jesus said, *"and sin no more."* This is one of the responsibilities that come with forgiveness.

The crowd that day had come to do just what Jesus said the devil comes to do: *"to steal, and to kill, and to destroy"* (John 10:10), but Jesus came that day to do just what He always does, and that is to offer us *"life ... more abundantly"* (also from John 10:10). The spirit of man is always present to condemn and bring down, to point the finger. The heart of man is set to respond to the sin nature, never to willingly walk in the spirit. Thank God for Jesus, for He forgives and gives the repentant man and woman the freedom (and responsibility) to rely on the Holy Spirit to guide them through life victorious over sin and the works of darkness.

JESUS SET THE EXAMPLE

Jesus set the example that guides the Church to understand that none of us can escape the destructive power of the evil one without a solid foundation in the Holy Spirit and without having our weapons of spiritual warfare. Paul warned the Church:

Neither give place to the devil.   Ephesians 4:27

We can keep him out by being well fortified against him. This is not to say that we will not be forgiven again if we fail to conduct ourselves perfectly. God knows our frailties, and He is ever ready to forgive. But, because He wants the very best for our lives, He calls us higher, to a life of responsibility and accountability.

OUR RESPONSIBILITY TO OTHERS

There are other aspects of our responsibility. One of them is to forgive as we have been forgiven. This will be covered in detail in Part III of the book. There are other ways we can show our gratitude to God, other responsibilities that come to us when we have been forgiven. The story of Zacchaeus teaches us more of these truths.

HOW THE RICH ARE TO RESPOND

And, behold, there was a man named Zacchaeus, which was the chief among the publicans, and he was rich. And he sought to see Jesus who he was; and could not for the press, because he was little of stature.

Luke 19:2-3

> **God's gift of forgiveness is for everyone, rich and poor alike!**

God's gift of forgiveness is for everyone, rich and poor alike. Too often the rich have only rich friends and consider the poor to be their enemies, but the Bible records the fact that Jesus changed the heart of this particular rich man, and, as a consequence, the poor became his friends. The man in question was Zacchaeus, a tax collector, and he was forgiven by Jesus because he repented of his false dealings and demonstrated the spirit of responsibility and accountability, thus gaining freedom from guilt and condemnation.

HAVING A LOOK AT THE MASTER

Many people want to have a look at the Master, but most rich people don't want to get so close that their deeds come to the light. Many, like Zacchaeus, are willing, at least, to take a quick look. They have heard of Jesus, and they're curious about Him. Others keep their distance because they're superstitious and don't want to be "exposed" or they've heard that the power of God is greater than the power of evil, and they decide to stay far enough away to remain "safe" because they have gained their wealth by evil means and are afraid that it might be jeopardized if they get too close to Truth. Zacchaeus felt compelled to see Jesus that day, and amazing things happened .

SUDDEN REPENTANCE IN THE PRESENCE OF GOD

And he ran before, and climbed up into a sycamore tree to see him: for he was to pass that way. And when Jesus came to the place, he looked up, and saw him, and said unto him, Zacchaeus, make hast, and come down; for to-day I must abide at thy house. And he made haste, and came down, and received him joyfully.

Luke 19:4-6

In the presence of Jesus, there is power to convict and to heal. Remarkably, without Jesus having to say a word about his evil past, this rich man suddenly became repentant and began to confess and surrender his will to the Lord. We believe that we have to do a lot of preaching and convincing of sinners, when often the Holy Spirit wants us to remain silent in humility and allow Him to work. After all, His ability is so unlimited, and ours is so limited.

Zacchaeus was lost, but Jesus saw that he would be

willing to forsake all and to repent and seek forgiveness in the presence of everyone. Thank God that this rich man was not ashamed to confess his sins that day.

No sermon was preached, no prayer was offered, and no charges were made against him by the Lord that day, and yet God moved upon his heart, and the Holy Ghost worked on his mind as he stood there in the presence of Jesus:

> *And Zacchaeus stood, and said unto the Lord; Behold, Lord, the half of my goods I give to the poor; and if I have taken any thing from any man by false accusation, I restore him fourfold.* Luke 19:8

A FRIEND OF THE POOR

In the process of all of this, Zacchaeus became a friend of Jesus and, consequently, a friend of the poor. His salvation came, and with it came responsibility and accountability. His riches and his wealth now found their proper place in his life.

Jesus concluded that salvation had come to the house of Zacchaeus, but it had come with a price. This is not to say that Zacchaeus needed to buy his salvation, but rather that, with it, he received a new responsibility and a new accountability, even as he rejoiced in his newfound freedom from guilt and condemnation.

Without anyone saying a word, the Holy Spirit moved upon his heart and showed him that he was responsible for helping the poor. This was not a temporary matter. He would be expected to maintain a spirit of compassion and charity toward those in need throughout his lifetime, as long as God was blessing him with more than enough for his own needs. This is an example to all who are rich and yet refuse to face their responsibility and be accountable to God and to their fellowmen.

That day Jesus insisted on dining at Zacchaeus' house, and He did it so that everyone would understand that, among the forgiven, rich and poor alike are one in Christ.

THE DO-NOTHING RICH MAN

In comparison to this story, in another chapter of Luke, Jesus spoke about those who do nothing to help others. A do-nothing rich man and a do-nothing unjust steward were, He showed us, to receive the same condemnation. First, let's look at the do-nothing rich man:

There was a certain rich man, which was clothed in purple and fine linen, and fared sumptuously every day: and there was a certain beggar named Lazarus, which was laid at his gate, full of sores, and desiring to be fed with the crumbs which fell from the rich man's table: moreover the dogs came and licked his sores.

Luke 16:19-21

Amazingly, Jesus said that this rich man would not have been persuaded to change, even if someone had preached to him about his responsibility. What was his responsibility? His first responsibility was to repent, and the second was to show mercy. Repentance was to be exercised toward God, and mercy and compassion were to

45

be exercised toward the poor. As Jesus taught earlier in His ministry:

*Thou shalt love the Lord thy God with all thy heart ...
and thou shalt love thy neighbour as thyself.*
Matthew 22:37 and 39

These two always go together.

As it happened, both the men in the story died, but the end of each was quite different:

*It came to pass, that the beggar died, and was carried
by the angels into Abraham's bosom: the rich man also
died, and was buried; and in hell he lifted up his eyes,
being in torments, and seeth Abraham afar off, and
Lazarus in his bosom.*
Luke 16:22-23

The rich man went to Hell, but not because he was rich. It was, rather, because he did nothing. He did nothing about his salvation, and he did nothing to help the poor. If he had given to the poor and neglected his own soul, his end would still have been the same. Salvation cannot be purchased with good works. Rather, salvation produces good works in us.

Can we call this rich man "wicked"? Yes, I think we can, and the Bible bears me out on this:

*The wicked shall be turned into hell, and all the nations
that forget God.*
Psalm 9:17

This rich man went to Hell because he was *"wicked."*

He was *"wicked"* because he refused to attend to his own soul and because he refused to extend aid to the poor when it was clearly within his power to do so. Unless they repent, those who are in authority in rich nations and turn their backs on God and His children are *"wicked"* and will be consigned to Hell for all eternity.

LENDING TO THE LORD

Many of us have to repent for doing wrong things, but others must repent for doing nothing with the abilities with which God has endowed us. One of those failures is to relieve some of the suffering in the world around us—both spiritually and physically:

> *He that hath pity upon the poor lendeth unto the LORD; and that which he hath given will he pay him again.*
>
> Proverbs 19:17

> *He was "wicked" because he refused to attend to his own soul and because he refused to extend aid to the poor!*

We can easily reverse this phrase and come to the conclusion that when we fail to give, when God has positioned us with the resources to do so, we are refusing to lend to God, and He will take from us double what we should have given in the first place.

SOME JUST DON'T CARE

Some people just don't care, and this seems to have been the attitude of the man Jesus called *"the unjust steward."* God had given him knowledge and ability to help those who were in need, but he didn't do it because he didn't care what happened to them. He had no fear of God and no compassion for suffering humanity.

This is just the opposite of another man whom Jesus lauded in the same passage:

> *His lord said unto him, Well done, thou good and faithful servant: thou hast been faithful over a few things, I will make thee ruler over any things: enter thou into the joy of thy lord.* Matthew 25:21

When we use what God, in His mercy, has given us, we will surely receive a commendation from the Lord Himself. When we refuse, we will be as the unjust steward:

> *Then he which had received the one talent came and said, Lord, I knew thee that thou art an hard man, reaping where thou hast not sown, and gathering where thou has not strawed: and I was afraid, and went and hid thy talent in the earth: lo, there thou hast that is thine.* Matthew 25:24-25

The confession of this man shows that he knew that whatever each of us has in this world is given to us by the merciful, generous and loving hand of God. We are only stewards of whatever has been placed in our hands, whether it be financial blessings or professional abilities. All that we own belongs to Almighty God:

> *Thus saith the LORD, The heaven is my throne, and the earth is my footstool.*   Isaiah 66:1

The answer of the Lord to the unjust steward was final. He had lived his entire lifetime in selfishness, and Jesus showed Him no mercy:

> *His lord answered and said unto him, Thou wicked and slothful servant.*   Matthew 25:26

Why was he called *"wicked"*? Because he did nothing. What he could have done and should have done was left undone. This shows that the sin of omission is equal to wickedness in God's sight. In finality, Jesus said:

> *And cast ye the unprofitable servant into outer darkness: there shall be weeping and gnashing of teeth.*
>   Matthew 25:30

Wow! That's serious.

Now, which of these characters do you more closely identify with, the forgiven righteous or the wicked man?

We can sum up the message of these examples, the woman forgiven for her adultery but admonished to *"go and sin no more"* and the rich man and unjust steward who were judged for their failure to aid the poor, when God, in His mercy, extends His forgiveness to us, a certain process must take place. Our understanding of sin must come to line up with God's hatred for rebellion and wickedness. Whereas there was in us before a love for the works of evil, now there must be a love for righteousness and obedience to the Word of God and a hatred for evil. We feel a new responsibility, to God and to our fellowman.

It is a blessing to be accounted worthy, as we obey the command of Jesus to watch and pray without ceasing, and concentrate on *Always Being Ready* for the Rapture.

CHAPTER 4

THE STRUGGLES
OF THE RICH AND FAMOUS

And after certain days, when Felix came with his wife Drusilla, which was a Jewess, he sent for Paul, and heard him concerning the faith in Christ. And as he reasoned of righteousness, temperance, and judgment to come, Felix trembled, and answered, Go thy way for this time; when I have a convenient season, I will call for thee.

Acts 24:24-25

Even though God's gift of repentance and forgiveness is extended to all men, the rich and famous often have a struggle with the humility that is required. The conviction to repent is a work of the Holy Spirit in us, and the means He uses is the power of the Word of God. Some men, however, upon hearing it, tremble and yet still fail to repent. This was the case of Felix, Governor of Judea in the time of the apostle Paul.

NOBLE?

Paul addressed Felix as *"noble"* (Acts 24:3), even though he was the husband of three queens or royal ladies, and the record of his actions includes all sorts of cruelty and lust in the exercise of his power over slaves. According to *Unger's Bible Dictionary* (Moody Press: 1985, page 405), he considered himself to have a license to

> **Even though God's gift of repentance and forgiveness is extended to all men, the rich and famous often have a struggle with the humility that is required.**

commit any crime, and he relied on the influence he had in the courts to escape punishment.

The apostle Paul was sent by the Lord to present the Gospel to this man, and Felix came very close to surrendering that day. In the end, however, all he did was tremble in fear at the power of the Holy Spirit through the Word of the Gospel, and that's not nearly enough. He, like many great men, was able to shrug off the convicting power of the Holy Spirit and go on in his own ways.

There is coming a time, however, when men who have refused to repent before God (great and small, rich and poor alike) will find themselves in terror:

> *And the kings of the earth, and the great men, and the rich men, and the chief captains, and the mighty men, and every bondman, and every free man, hid themselves in the dens and in the rocks of the mountains; and said to the mountains and rocks, Fall on us, and hide us from the face of him that sitteth on the throne, and from the wrath of the Lamb: for the great day of his wrath is come; and who shall be able to stand?*
>
> Revelation 6:15-17

Why would any man want to wait to repent until the great day of God's wrath, when there will be no hope of escape? Great men (just like ordinary men) can turn to the Lord now, and they can do it, not because of fear, but because of truth. The truth is that Jesus is coming again, and we have two choices: surrendering to God's will and rising with Him in the air or experiencing His wrath.

God did not appoint His children to wrath:

For God hath not appointed us to wrath, but to obtain salvation by our Lord Jesus Christ.

1 Thessalonians 5:9

The Rapture, therefore, will be history by the time the seven years of the Great Tribulation begin, when the Lamb of God will appear to fight His enemies. We who love Him will be long gone. Why would anyone risk not being ready for that great day?

FELIX'S OPPORTUNITY

According to the book of Acts, Felix had the opportunity to settle for the First Resurrection (which will take place before the Rapture of the Church), but he chose to remain a wicked man until his death. This is sad because he was clearly brought to the point of repentance, but he resisted and chose to continue in his evil.

This is not some judgmental conclusion. The biblical record shows very clearly that after that day Felix never again called upon Paul in order to submit himself to the Gospel, but rather to try to use his evil influence to extort money for the apostle's release:

He hoped also that money should have been given him of Paul, that he might loose him: wherefore he sent for him the oftener, and communed with him.

Acts 24:26

Historians have it right. Felix was a man of lust for money and pleasure. For the next two years he tried to persuade the apostle Paul to raise money to pay him off to be released from prison. Paul, however, being a man of great integrity and holiness, refused to bow to this evil. He was not guilty of any crime; he was only being persecuted for preaching the Gospel.

Thank God for the presence of Jesus with Paul. This man had been sent to preach and also to demonstrate the Gospel to Felix with a life of righteousness, and part of his demonstration was that a Christian is a soldier of the cross and must *"endure hardness"* as such (2 Timothy 2:3).

Sadly, Felix did not respond positively to Paul's message. Great men seem to be easily hardened in their hearts and find it difficult, if not impossible, to bow before God and repent. Eventually, Felix's opportunity passed:

But after two years Porcius Festus came into Felix'
room: and Felix, willing to shew the Jews a pleasure,
left Paul bound.   Acts 24:27

Felix had his chance, but he "blew it." His first hearing of the Gospel had caused him to tremble with conviction and desire, but he had brushed it off. And even though he often spoke with Paul after that, his thoughts were more on the bribes he hoped to receive than on the truth of Christ and the good of his own soul. How sad!

WHAT IT TAKES FOR A
FAMOUS AND POWERFUL MAN TO REPENT

The rich and famous do occasionally repent, but it usually takes humiliation to bring them to it. A good

55

example from ancient history was one of its most powerful kings—Nebuchadnezzar of Babylon. As a rich and powerful ruler, this man had committed many sins, but regardless of what a person has done, they are never beyond the supernatural ability of God to forgive and restore. The Scriptures ask the rhetorical question:

Is any thing too hard for the LORD?   Genesis 18:14

The answer, of course, is: No! Nothing is too hard for Him. However, we must say that the presence of riches, power and influence have always made it difficult for men to repent.

It is no different today than it was in the time of Nebuchadnezzar. Wealth and power somehow become obstacles to humility and obedience to the laws of righteousness. This is why Jesus said:

Verily I say unto you, That a rich man shall hardly enter into the kingdom of heaven. And again I say unto you, It is easier for a camel to go through the eye of a needle, than for a rich man to enter into the kingdom of God.   Matthew 19:23-24

But, again, we must insist, as God's Word declares, that He can do the otherwise impossible:

Ah Lord GOD! behold, thou hast made the heaven and the earth by thy great power and stretched out arm, and there is nothing too hard for thee.
                                    Jeremiah 32:17

THE ROOT OF ALL EVIL

Even the poor must seek forgiveness from the Lord when they have been caught up in the ugly web of seeking riches by squandering their meager income on get-rich-quick schemes and gambling, especially playing the lottery. Paul warned:

> *For the love of money is the root of all evil: which while some coveted after, they have erred from the faith, and pierced themselves through with many sorrows.*
>
> 1 Timothy 6:10

Wealth and power somehow become obstacles to humility and obedience to the laws of righteousness!

Note the word *all* in the phrase *"the root of all evil."* That makes this a very important point. Instead of playing the lottery with the false hope of hitting a jackpot, the poor would be more blessed if they used part of their small income to relieve the suffering of the less fortunate in the poorer countries. God sees the heart, and the tragic truth is that even many Christians cannot be prosperous because they make wrong choices. Greed for power and wealth is one of the works of the flesh that has brought much misery and pain to mankind, more perhaps than any other evil under the sun.

BLINDED BY WEALTH

King Nebuchadnezzar was blinded by the wealth he controlled, but when he was humbled, he accepted the fact that his sins and iniquity had forced God to bring judgment upon him. Was he brought so low that he was *forced* to repent? Not really. Many great men are humbled, and it doesn't seem to do anything for their attitude. When Nebuchadnezzar came to the knowledge of his sinfulness, he realized that God was Lord of all and rules—even in the hearts of men. The Scriptures record that God used this man, even calling him a servant, but the same was never said of Felix.

Nebuchadnezzar's restoration did not come easily. It took seven years of humiliation, loneliness and rejection to bring him to his knees, to a place of repentance and turning to God:

> *And at the end of the days [seven years] I Nebuchadnezzar lifted up mine eyes unto heaven, and mine understanding returned unto me, and I blessed the most High, and I praised and honoured him that liveth for ever, whose dominion is an everlasting dominion, and his kingdom is from generation to generation.*
>
> Daniel 4:34

Thankfully, the story of Nebuchadnezzar had a happy ending. Sadly, the story of Felix did not.

THREE WOMEN AND THREE DISASTERS FOR SAMSON

Felix and Nebuchadnezzar were both secular leaders, but this very same principle applies to spiritual leaders as well. Samson was one of the great men of Israel in the early days of the conquest of Canaan. He was God's chosen servant to lead the nation as judge. Still, as great as he was in many ways, Samson fell into the powerful sins of the lust of the flesh and the lust of the eyes. The three women in his life were all wrong choices. Still, in the end, Samson repented and was forgiven.

WOMAN #1:

Samson lost his first wife when she was burned to death by the Philistines:

> *Then the Philistines said, Who hath done this? [Samson had burned their fields of corn.] And they answered, Samson, the son in law of the Timnite, because he had taken his wife, and given her to his companion. And the Philistines came up, and burnt her and her father with fire.*   Judges 15:6

That was the end of Samson's first marriage.

WOMAN #2

Next, Samson *"went in unto"* *"a harlot"*:

> *Then went Samson to Gaza, and saw there an harlot, and went in unto her.*   Judges 16:1

This reprehensible act represented a typical downward spiral that great men (and small) often follow when, for one reason or another, they're out of the perfect will of God. They suddenly find the freedom to do whatever their flesh prompts them to do at the moment.

Samson fell from being a mighty, respected and honored man of God to being a reviled and tortured prisoner of his enemies!

Unfortunately, Samson continued downward into this deep pit of pleasure. There was certainly a point at which he could have stopped his bad behavior and averted destruction, but when our heart is not willing to stop and question our actions, or when we refuse to seek or follow the counsel of the wise or to stop and seek the mind of God on a given subject, it then becomes impossible to avoid descending further on that slippery slope.

Samson was headed for a serious fall.

WOMAN #3

And it came to pass afterward, that he loved a woman in the valley of Sorek, whose name was Delilah.

Judges 16:4

The next woman in Samson's life was Delilah. The meaning of this Hebrew name is "tease," and Delilah was the bait the devil used to bring Samson into bondage to his enemies. He was about to lose something extremely valuable, and he didn't even know it:

And she made him sleep upon her knees; and she called for a man, and she caused him to shave off the seven locks of his head; and she began to afflict him, and his strength went from him. ... The Philistines took him, and put out his eyes, and brought him down to Gaza, and bound him with fetters of brass; and he did grind in the prison house. Judges 16:19 and 21

Samson fell from being a mighty, respected and honored man of God to being a reviled and tortured prisoner of his enemies. Adultery can be deadly, and the punishment for it is irreversible, unless repentance changes the course of things.

SAMSON'S RESTORATION

Did God forgive Samson when he repented? Yes, of course. The sad thing is that his repentance came only after he had been imprisoned, blinded and tortured. Did God grant him his desires after his repentance? Yes, He did, and we cannot minimize that fact, but it did come very late in the game:

And Samson called unto the LORD, and said, O Lord God, remember me, I pray thee, and strengthen me, I pray thee, only this once, O God, that I may be at once avenged of the Philistines for my two eyes.

Judges 16:28

God answered that prayer because Samson repented, and, with these short and simple phrases, he was restored back to fellowship with the Almighty.

Men who think they are great and don't need God will have to learn the hard way the biblical truth of Proverbs:

Pride goeth before destruction, and an haughty spirit before a fall. Better it is to be of an humble spirit with the lowly, than to divide the spoil with the proud.

Proverbs 16:18-19

We can only hope that their fall will cause in them the right reaction: a search for peace and purpose. The moment they begin to hunger and thirst for peace, mercy and true joy, the Spirit of God will come to lead them to the reservoir of God's peace, and there they can receive God's forgiveness and a new life in Christ. At that moment, their purpose for living will be changed from a life of self-centeredness to a mission of bringing hope to a dying world.

How about you? Are fame and riches holding you back from obeying God? The Holy Spirit, through the apostle Paul, admonishes the believers to comfort one another with these words, as we all concentrate on *Always Being Ready.*

CHAPTER 5

WHAT ABOUT DIVORCE?

When a man hath taken a wife, and married her, and it come to pass that she find no favour in his eyes, because he hath found some uncleanness in her: then let him write her a bill of divorcement, and give it in her hand, and send her out of his house.

Deuteronomy 24:1

As we have seen, Jesus forgave what we consider to

be one of the worst sins, adultery. What about divorce? Is there forgiveness for divorce? Can a person who has divorced and remarried experience life again, life without guilt and condemnation? Can God use a divorced person?

TWIN ENEMIES OF THE FAMILY

Divorce and adultery have been two of the enemies of marriage and the family for many generations. These destructive forces came about because of the Fall of man and his subsequent imperfection. In God's eyes, it would have been better if divorce had never occurred. He hates it. But, with the same token, His power to forgive what causes it has no limits. His grace is without measure and is, therefore, sufficient for every situation.

DIVORCE AND ADULTERY ARE TWO VERY DIFFERENT THINGS

Let's be clear. Divorce and adultery are two very different things. Divorce is a legal matter. It represents a recognized separation between a man and his wife. Adultery, however, is a sin. Sin may be the reason for a divorce, but the divorce, in itself, is not necessarily a sin. For example, not divorcing your spouse is not one of the Ten Commandments.

Even though the consequences of divorce can be disastrous, divorce itself was never called a sin in the Bible. It is men who have focused so much on divorce and tried to place condemnation on those who have suffered its ravages. Adultery brings God's condemnation on the adulterer, and, in Old Testament times, was punishable by death. This, however, was never true of divorce. And, although adultery may be grounds for divorce, there are other causes of divorce as well. The Law of Moses was very liberal in this matter, but it was not equal.

NOT EQUAL

The Law was not equal in its treatment of men and women when it came to divorce. It gave most rights to the man and nearly none to the woman. Under the Law, men did the divorcing, fair or not.

Jesus never condemned divorce or divorced people. A Samaritan woman, whom He encountered at the well one day (see John 4:16-18), had already had five husbands, and yet He spoke kindly to her and offered her eternal life. How could she have gotten away with so many divorces? The Law was for the Jews, so it didn't apply to her case, for it had no jurisdiction over the Samaritans. A Samaritan woman could divorce as many times as she pleased, just as a man could. Under Moses' Law, only the men had this freedom. Still, fair or not, neither the man nor the woman were punished for divorce or even called upon to repent of it.

> *Sin may be the reason for a divorce, but the divorce, in itself, is not necessarily a sin!*

When Jesus came, He denounced divorce as practiced under the Law and pointed out that it had been put into practice because of the hardness of the hearts of the people. Still, even though it had been a one-sided and unfair practice, He didn't call it a sin. We never say that a person has "committed divorce," but we do say that a person has "committed adultery":

> *And the man that committeth adultery with another man's wife, even he that committeth adultery with his neighbour's wife, the adulterer and the adulteress shall surely be put to death.*   Leviticus 20:10

God's standard of righteousness is unchanged today, but men have added divorce to the list of serious offenses.

JESUS FORGAVE ADULTERY

As we noted in a previous chapter, when the woman caught in the act of adultery was brought to Jesus, He forgave her (see John 8:11). The shamefulness of this sin had not changed from Old Testament to New Testament times. Just as Jesus is the same yesterday, today and forever, so also is His righteousness and His holiness. Still, He forgave.

And Jesus, who forgave this woman caught in the act of adultery (and this was before He had shed His precious blood on the cross of Calvary), is the same Jesus who can forgive the person who has committed the sin of adultery in modern times, long after His blood was shed for all sin. If you fall victim to this temptation, remember that you are not alone. Millions of others have been right where you are, and many of them have found peace through the wonderful and powerful grace of God, and are now again living the abundant life in Christ. If you have divorced and remarried, it may not be God's very best plan for your life, but it will, in no way, keep you out of Heaven.

THE UNFORGIVING CHURCH

The unforgiving church today is just like the pharisaical priest and the Pharisees who came to Jesus, condemning the woman taken in adultery. Many modern books on this subject of divorce and remarriage condemn rather than enlighten those who are seeking to hear what Christ's position is on the matter. Many take the position of the Pharisees, willing and ready to kill the woman rather than restore her, as Jesus did. In all that people like this do, the power of God's love is never preached. This pharisaical position does not present Jesus as the One who came not *"to condemn the world, but that the world through him might be saved"* (John 3:17).

DAVID'S PREMEDITATED ADULTERY AND MURDER

Did David know what he was about to do when it came to Bathsheba? If he hadn't had time to learn that the woman he was about to go to bed with was someone else's wife, he definitely did have time to meditate on the sinfulness of his act and didn't seem to care what the cost might be. In that moment, his lust needed to be satisfied, for it was ruling his heart.

This relationship with Bathsheba involved two married persons, and when David decided to have her husband killed to cover up his wrongdoing, his sin deepened to the point of adultery and premeditated murder.

> **Jesus commanded this woman to turn away from adultery as a pattern of life and to begin living a holy life!**

This was further complicated when he involved others in his scheme to kill the innocent man. Not only were his hands now stained with blood, but also the hands of Joab, his Commander (see 2 Samuel 11:14-15 and 17-18).

WHERE WAS THE MAN?

We know that the woman who was brought to Jesus and accused of adultery was married, or she would not have been accused of this sin. Whoever the man was, he had to have been a married man as well. Why didn't they bring him to Jesus too? He was just as guilty as she was.

There is no higher law regarding adultery in the New Testament as opposed to the Old Testament, but there is greater grace for the offence, once the offender is willing to repent and do as Jesus commanded the woman: *"Go, and sin no more"* (John 8:11). In other words, Jesus commanded this woman to turn away from adultery as a pattern of life and to begin living a holy life. There is a difference between an act of adultery and a life of adultery:

Jesus answered them, Verily, verily, I say unto you, Whosoever committeth sin is the servant of sin.

John 8:34

This was the difference in David's case. He refused to be *"the servant of sin."* Instead, he married Bathsheba and lived with her, after their adulterous affair, not as a condemned man, but as a forgiven saint of God. He was still *"a man after his [God's] own heart"* (1 Samuel 13:14).

YOU HAVE HOPE

If our Lord and Savior is the same yesterday, today and forever (and we know that He is), then there must be hope for those who have fallen into the sin of adultery. Our God never changes, and if He was a God of mercy to David, then, based on His Word, He remains even now faithful to His divine nature. This is why Samson (a philanderer) and David were both forgiven, restored, filled with the Holy Spirit and then mightily used by God. As David sang:

For thou, Lord, art good, and ready to forgive; and plenteous in mercy unto all them that call upon thee.

Psalm 86:5

Self-righteous men usually judge people by what they

see, but God knows the heart. If premeditated adultery and murder can be forgiven by Him, is there any sin on earth that He would not or cannot forgive (except the sin of blasphemy against the Holy Spirit)? So remember today: please do not condemn yourself and refuse to receive condemnation from others. Only Christ has the right to condemn a man or woman, and He'll never condemn you.

Don't trust what men say about this subject. Go to Christ, and set your hope on His return. Only Jesus can deliver you from oppression and depression. Thank God for His unspeakable gift and the power of His redeeming love. Be sure you have repented and then live in the glow of God's forgiveness.

DAVID AND BATHSHEBA WERE BLESSED

David and Bathsheba went on to be blessed:

And David comforted Bath-sheba his wife, and went in unto her, and lay with her: and she bare a son, and he called his name Solomon: and the LORD loved him.

2 Samuel 12:24

There is no further record of the life of the woman caught in the act of adultery and forgiven by Jesus, but I believe that no one who comes to Him, repents and is forgiven can ever walk away without the desire (and the power) to live a consistent righteous life. Therefore I believe that this woman, who had been caught in the act of adultery, followed Jesus faithfully the rest of her life. He knew she would, and that's why He forgave her.

The command that Jesus gave the accused woman that day, *"go and sin no more,"* is the same command He gives you and all who will come to Him. When He sent her away that day, she was not condemned. Instead, she was given this divine charge. She was now free to live, like David, in a new relationship if she chose to do so, only in the Lord.

ALL THREE POSSIBLE PATHS
REQUIRE REPENTANCE AND FORGIVENESS

Once the damage of adultery has been done, there is nothing anyone can do about the past. There are, however, three possible paths for the future. One of these possible paths is reconciliation with the offended marriage partner. A second possible path is a new relationship. And the third possible path is to remain unmarried for life. Regardless of which path a person pursues, their prayer for repentance must be offered, and forgiveness must be granted. This will set the soul free to move forward without guilt and remorse. There is forgiveness with God. David sang:

> *Out of the depths have I cried unto thee, O LORD. Lord, hear my voice: let thine ears be attentive to the voice of my supplications. If thou, LORD, shouldest mark iniquities, O Lord, who shall stand? But there is forgiveness with thee, that thou mayest be feared.*
>
> Psalm 130:1-4

No matter how great our sinfulness may be, God's grace and mercy is sufficient to restore us. However there must be repentance and forgiveness, for this is the necessary foundation for *any* path that is to be taken in the future. If your chosen path is reconciliation, there must first be repentance and forgiveness. If you choose to be in a new relationship, there must be repentance and forgiveness. And even if you choose to spend the rest of your life unmarried, repentance and forgiveness are necessary to restore you to the proper relationship with God.

APPLYING THE GRACE OF GOD TO YOUR SITUATION

Repentance and forgiveness have the effect of applying the grace of God to your situation and restoring peace of mind and the fullness of joy to your spirit. Your strength now comes from the power of the work of the cross.

There is no such thing as being more forgiven or less forgiven. Forgiveness is the removal of the punishment and guilt attached to the crime, and once it is gone (and that's what happens in forgiveness), it is gone forever. And gone means gone. As far as God is concerned, it should never be remembered against you again.

DEALING WITH PEOPLE WHO KNOW YOUR PAST

If you have committed adultery or been divorced for some other reason, you will almost certainly be judged by others. But no one knows your heart like Jesus. The forgiveness He has extended to you came at a great price, and you don't have to justify your life to anyone ever again. You have laid your burden on Him, and so you don't have to carry it any longer.

Now that you have the joy of the Lord restored to your dying soul, no one can take that away from you. Once His forgiveness has set you free, your only charge is to keep moving with Christ and follow Him daily.

This doesn't mean that you will be perfect. You were not perfect before you were forgiven, and you will not be perfect after the Lord has lifted the load off your shoulders. But are you on the same level as those who have an unblemished marriage? In the eyes of man, no, you're not, but in the eyes of God, yes, you are.

Yes! Yes! Yes! A million times yes! In God's eyes, we are all sinners saved by grace, and you will now be welcomed into His presence when you pray, just like any other saint of God.

Will God answer your prayers? Of course He will. Lack of forgiveness can hinder your prayers, and

> *Repentance and forgiveness have the effect of applying the grace of God to your situation and restoring peace of mind and the fullness of joy to your spirit!*

sins of willful rebellion will do the same, but Jesus said, *"Blessed are the meek"* (Matthew 5:5). Remember, you are one of millions who have suffered this destructive strategic spiritual warfare from the Prince of Darkness, and God's plan for you is not based on what you have done, but on the work He accomplished on Calvary.

In Christ, the divorcee has not lost his or her position with God, for we are each in His family, not based on what we have done or not done for Him, but on what He has done for us. You can only lose your position in Christ if you willingly turn your back on Him and become a servant of the devil, an unbeliever. As long as your faith is in the work that Christ has done on the cross, you can rest assured that He is with you.

JESUS' ATTITUDE TOWARD DIVORCE

When Jesus was confronted with the question of divorce, He said that this choice of a man and woman for settling their differences had been allowed under the Law because of the hardness of the people's hearts:

> *They say unto him [Jesus], Why did Moses then command to give a writing of divorcement, and to put her away? He [Jesus] saith unto them, Moses because of the hardness of your hearts suffered you to put away your wives: but from the beginning it was not so.*
>
> Matthew 19:7-8

Even though Jesus gave this answer, He knew that when He went to the cross He would die for the redemption of man's hardened heart and for those who had become victims of this destructive sin. Thank God for the power of the cross and His shed blood. Still, He never said that divorce was a sin, especially not the sin of blasphemy against the Holy Ghost, as some mistakenly claim. It's not.

TAKING AUTHORITY IN YOUR SITUATION

Once you have repented and have been forgiven, you are in command and can then take authority to wage spiritual warfare on behalf of your victorious future. This time, as you look to the future, you will use the whole armor of God. Everywhere and every time the enemy attacks, you will be ready.

Sometimes you'll feel guilty. That's the devil's work and he's very good at it. No matter what fault you may have and no matter what you have done, this is your challenge—to hold on to your deliverance with joy. You are walking in God's gift of the abundant life through the power of the Holy Spirit. Don't let go of that for any reason.

Thank God that Jesus is not a man, but the Son of God. He took my sins and your sins to Calvary, and He did not discriminate. Jews, as well as Gentiles, have access to the throneroom of the grace of an almighty and holy God.

DEALING WITH MATTHEW 19:9

It is true that Jesus, in Matthew 19:9, compared

divorce and remarriage to the sin of adultery, yet He forgave the woman who was caught in that very sin. If Jesus could forgive a woman of such sins even before He went to Calvary, how much more will He forgive any man or woman caught up in adultery after He has shed His blood for all the sins of the world on the cross! That should settle the matter forever.

> *Jesus refused to condemn her, and she was the only one who walked away from the Lord that day free from condemnation!*

THAT SPIRITUAL CHIP ON MY SHOULDER

When the accused woman was brought by the scribes and Pharisees to Jesus, He proved that they were hypocrites, for here they were accusing a woman of sin, when they themselves were just as sinful as she or perhaps even worse. Religion is like that, full of hypocrisy, and this can be said of many Christian churches today. May God forgive us for the chip on our shoulders!

These men came to Jesus with a spiritual chip on their shoulders. They came telling Him what this woman had done, but they were not willing to shed light on all that *they* had done wrong. Jesus refused to condemn her, and she was the only one who walked away from the Lord that day free from condemnation.

BUT CAN GOD STILL USE ME?

Only God can change the heart of a man or woman, but He can. His Word declares that He will remove *"the stony heart"* from man and give him *"a heart of flesh"*:

And I will give them one heart, ... and I will take the stony heart out of their flesh, and will give them an heart of flesh: that they may walk in my statutes, and keep mine ordinances, and do them: and they shall be my people, and I will be their God. Ezekiel 11:19-20

This *"heart of flesh"* represents the spirit of a merciful and forgiving believer. Let God do this miracle for you today.

There is abundant life after divorce and forgiveness. You may not be the person who caused the offence. But regardless of who was guilty, God has enough grace and Calvary's love is deep and wide enough to restore that person and everyone else involved. And, yes, God can use you again.

Did David minister after he was forgiven for adultery and murder? Of course he did. He was used mightily by God in many different ways and is remembered as a man after God's own heart.

The Spirit of God is available to all those who hunger and thirst for Him. It is not required that they be pre-fect, only forgiven. The unforgiving and self-righteous will say, "God can't use you because your testimony is all messed up," but the truth is that God delights in using broken vessels. After David had committed adultery and premeditated murder, he could say that God was still using him to teach transgressors His ways and to bring sinners to conversion (see Psalm 51). Who, then, is to say that God can't do that very same thing for any man or woman who comes to Him with a broken and contrite spirit?

GOD CAN USE YOUR TESTIMONY

I have news for those who speak from their self-righteousness. God can use the testimony of our past and our deliverance from it for His glory. If you are filled with the Spirit of God, the Word of God that you preach to sinners will be used to speak to them, and the Holy Spirit will then draw them to God and deliver them.

Regardless of what men may say about your testimony, the Lord says that there is nothing too hard for Him. It is impossible to correct or change the past, and far too many spend their time regretting it. That is wasted time. The only thing that we can change, with the power of God, is the future, so get headed in the right direction and stop worrying about the past.

There are many pastors and evangelists who themselves have suffered devastating damage to their lives and testimony due to marital problems, divorce and unfaithfulness, but in spite of these experiences and setbacks, these men and women are still being used by God in a mighty way. What else can they do but go right back to God, their Savior, seek forgiveness and receive from Him a mandate and plan for service for Him?

THE RIGHTEOUS DON'T STAY DOWN

No one should give up and throw in the towel just because the devil knocks them down one time. Righteous men and women never stay down. Instead, they rise up to prevail because God is in them and He cannot fail:

Lay not wait, O wicked man, against the dwelling of the righteous; spoil not his resting place: for a just man [or woman] falleth seven times, and riseth up again: but the wicked shall fall into mischief.

Proverbs 24:15-16

If there is to be life, it will be in the present and in the future, not in the past. So forget the past and move on.

BUILDING A SOLID MARRIAGE

Every marriage that has its foundation in Christ and the cross and is built on that Rock can stand the test of time. For any union that is forged in the will of God, there is hope. We must do our part to maintain a healthy marriage. No matter how hard Satan may try, if the Lord is building that house, it will not crash.

That is not a reason to become careless. Often the devil rears his ugly head in a man or woman after many years of marriage. Just because they said "I do" doesn't protect them from attack. The vast numbers of modern divorces, even among believers, proves this point.

But God is the God of the second chance, not the God of the second Hellhole. When He forgives the repentant sinner, He does not send them into the future to live in a second nightmare. Ideally, they are given the wisdom of the Holy Spirit to make God-ordained choices that will glorify His name. If someone ends up in a Hellhole of a relationship again, they got there on their own because God is not the author of confusion.

THE POWER OF THE CROSS IS MORE THAN ENOUGH

The power of God's mercy, His unfailing love and unbounded grace to deliver is more than enough to deliver anyone whom the enemy has attacked. We understand that even the ungodly know that these attacks upon the family can be devastating. What they do not know is that there is power in the work of the cross to deliver from all oppression and depression. The saints of God know the truth. Jesus came to destroy the works of the devil, and He did it through the cross and through His resurrection.

The signs of the times reveal that the Rapture is even now imminent. Christians must be consistently living in a state of repentance, forgiveness and readiness. As we see the day approaching, let us rejoice and be glad, as we concentrate on *Always Being Ready;* for great will be our reward in Heaven.

CHAPTER 6

FORGIVENESS FOR DEPARTING FROM GOD'S PERFECT WILL

For indeed he was sick nigh unto death: but God had mercy on him; and not on him only, but on me also, lest I should have sorrow upon sorrow.

Because for the work of Christ he was nigh unto death, not regarding his life [physical body], to supply your lack of service toward me. Philippians 2:27 and 30

Repentance and forgiveness work for the believer in every situation, and we must be quick to employ them as often as they are needed. It may be surprising to some that we can sometimes fail God and fall into trouble even when we are doing good, if the good we're doing doesn't happen to be the perfect will of God for us at the moment. Compassion for others sometimes prompts believers to do more than they can physically and spiritually handle. If we are walking in obedience to the Holy Spirit, through constantly praying and seeking God's divine plan and direction, we can save ourselves from a lot of unnecessary pain and anguish.

> *Repentance and forgiveness work for the believer in every situation, and we must be quick to employ them as often as they are needed!*

THE CASE OF EPAPHRODITUS

The experience of Epaphroditus, a companion of the apostle Paul, is an example worth examining in this regard. According to the record Paul left us, God had mercy on his companion, forgave Him and healed his sickness caused by overexertion.

Going beyond the divine will of God has been the error of many men and women of God, as they follow their zeal without sufficient knowledge, but in God's divine love and wisdom, He places limits and parameters that are there to enable us to remain within His perfect will. Many times, due to the power of the works of the flesh in our lives, we find ourselves committing the sin of Balaamism.

WHAT IS BALAAMISM?

Balaam's error is one that every believer should examine, for his sin is one that many men and women of God are committing today and then, rather than repent and seek forgiveness, they are attempting to justify their actions.

Balaam started out well, and this is revealed by what he said when his heart was in complete obedience to the Almighty:

> *And Balaam answered and said unto the servants of Balak, If Balak would give me his house of silver and gold, I cannot go beyond the word of the LORD my God, to do less or more.* Numbers 22:18

That sounded good, but in the very next verse, Balaam can be seen changing his position. What happened? It is apparent that his heart began to lust after the silver and gold, and he was tempted to consider the idea that maybe God would change *His* mind so that the prophet could be financially promoted. As a result, he disobeyed the Word of God, failing to understand that once God has spoken, there is no reason for Him to change His mind or take back what He has said. If God should decide to change His original command, He is just and holy enough to let His servants know that fact. Otherwise, His Word is irrevocable and irreversible.

Balaam's lust for the vainglory of man and his desire for pride and popularity cost him his life and a place among the prophets who passed the test and became spiritual role models for others during their lifetime. Just as Joseph has been a spiritual role model for young men and women for many centuries, so too, Balaam could have had his life exalted to the place of divine commendation. All he had to do was take God at His word and never doubt in his heart what God had originally said.

NEVER DOUBT GOD

Sometimes, however, God is not as practical as we would like Him to be. We must remember that His ways are *"higher than [our] ways"* and His thoughts are *"higher than [our] thoughts"*:

> *For my thoughts are not your thoughts, neither are your ways my ways, saith the LORD. For as the heavens are higher than the earth, so are my ways higher than your ways, and my thoughts than your thoughts.*
>
> Isaiah 55:8-9

We may not understand all that God does, but we are not asked to understand. We are called only to trust and obey Him—whether we understand or not.

We must never doubt God. Faith is taking God at His

word. Jesus is our example, and He pleased the Father because He was set in all His ways to do the Father's will—whatever the cost.

ACT ON TIME

When we err (and we do), God grants us time to repent, but some people use up their grace period, their time for repentance, and, sadly, they still fail to act and receive no extension from Heaven. This has been true from the beginning of time:

And the LORD said, My Spirit shall not always strive with man, for that he also is flesh: yet his days shall be an hundred and twenty years.   Genesis 6:3

There is a profound message in the way this verse is expressed in the Living Bible:

My Spirit must not forever be disgraced in man, wholly evil as he is. I will give him 120 years to mend his ways.
                              Genesis 6:3, TLB

This is what God said in the time of Noah, and when the one-hundred-and-twenty-year period ended, the flood came. Nothing could hold it back.

Too often people fail to realize that time quickly passes. It does not go on forever. The time we have to respond to the Word of God is always limited, so we cannot afford to put obedience off until tomorrow.

In the cases of Balaam, Herod, King Saul and King

Ahab, they all had space to repent and seek forgiveness from God. However, because it was not in their hearts to surrender and accept the fact that they had been wrong, they each continued in their rebellious ways and were rejected by God and eventually destroyed. God exercised His foreknowledge and brought His wrath and judgment upon them, because He knew they would never repent.

Taking chances with forgiveness and your eternal destiny is not wise. In fact, nothing could be more foolish. Again, it's like playing Russian Roulette with your soul.

FORGIVENESS IS BETWEEN GOD AND MAN

When it comes to repentance and forgiveness, no one can repent for you, and no one can seek forgiveness for you. Samuel, as we will see more in detail in the next chapter, tried to intercede for Saul, and he cried to God all night:

> *Then came the word of LORD unto Samuel, saying, It repenteth me that I have set up Saul to be king: for he is turned back from following me, and hath not performed my commandments. And it grieved Samuel; and he cried unto the LORD all night.*　　1 Samuel 15:10-11

In the end, the prophet could not save the soul of that king. If there was to be deliverance for King Saul, the words of repentance and the cries for mercy would have had to come from him, and he would have had to do it before it was too late. He refused, and therefore his end was sad.

No one can say for sure what would have happened if King Saul had turned to God within the grace period God had granted him for repentance and forgiveness. Only God knows.

We may sometimes go beyond the will of God doing that which is good, or we may go beyond the will of God doing that which is evil, as disobedience to His Word. God understands the desire to do good, as in the example of Epaphroditus, and He is always ready to forgive us through His abundant mercy. He is just as ready to forgive us when we err in wrongdoing. Sometimes the tests we face are severe.

> *Taking chances with forgiveness and your eternal destiny is not wise!*

A Startling Example

There is a very startling example that is worth considering here:

> *And the king said unto the man of God, Come home with me, and refresh thyself, and I will give thee a reward. And the man of God said unto the king, If thou wilt give me half thine house, I will not go in with thee, neither will I eat bread nor drink water in this place: for so was it charged me by the word of the Lord, saying, Eat no bread, nor drink water, nor turn again by the same way that thou camest. So he went another way, and returned not by the way that he came to Beth-el.*
>
> 1 Kings 13:7-10

So far this man of God had done very well, but we always experience tests in this life, and at no time can we simply relax and drift. Jesus said that we must take up our cross and follow Him daily, and this is the challenge of any soldier of the cross. Surprisingly, the temptation this prophet now faced came from another "prophet":

Now there dwelt an old prophet in Beth-el; and his sons came and told him all the works that the man of God had done that day in Beth-el: the words which he had spoken unto the king, them they told also to their father. And he said unto his sons, Saddle me the ass. So they saddled him the ass: and he rode thereon. And went after the man of God, and found him sitting under an oak: and he said unto him, Art thou the man of God that camest from Judah? And he said, I am. Then he said unto him, Come home with me, and eat bread.

1 Kings 13:11 and 13-15

A tragedy was about to befall the younger prophet, but why did it happen? Do we have a clue here? Is it meaningful that this man was found *"sitting under an oak"*? Does this, perhaps, indicate that he had given in to the flesh or stopped praying? Why was he just sitting there? We're not told any other details in the Scriptures. No reason is given for his having stopped. The lesson I take from this is that if we stop on our way home, it must always be for a spiritual rest, not for some fleshly reason.

This prophet refused to stop on his way to this mission, so maybe he should not have stopped on his way home from it either. Whatever the case, we must always be watchful and prayerful, as we listen to what others are saying to us. There's a reason the Scriptures declare:

Let God be true, but every man a liar.   Romans 3:4

EVEN SOME PROPHETS LIE, SO BE EXTRA VIGILANT AND SOBER

And he said, I may not return with thee, nor go in with thee: neither will I eat bread nor drink water with thee in this place. For it was said to me by the word of the LORD. ...
He said unto him, I am a prophet also as thou art; and an angel spake unto me by the word of the LORD, saying, Bring him back with thee into thine house, that he may eat bread and drink water. But he lied unto him. So he went back with him, and did eat bread in his house and drank water.   1 Kings 13:16-19

This younger prophet was approaching a point from which the opportunity of turning back for his deliverance would be lost forever. From that point on, until the end of his life, he would face God's irreversible judgment. He had passed a few of the tests presented to him, but he was now failing to pass one of the most important of them. Tragically, he failed just before he reached home. This should be a warning to us all. It's not only how we begin the race or how we run it; it's also extremely important how we finish this race:

> *Let God search you today, believe what He tells you, and return back to the path of the will of God by repenting and seeking His forgiveness!*

And it came to pass, as they sat at the table, that the word of the LORD came unto the prophet that brought him back: and he cried unto the man of God that came from Judah, saying, Thus saith the LORD, Forasmuch as thou has disobeyed the mouth of the LORD, and hast not kept the commandment which the LORD commanded thee, ... thy carcase shall not come unto the sepulchre of thy fathers. And when he was gone, a lion met him by the way, and slew him: and his carcase was cast in the way, and the ass stood by it, the lion also stood by the carcase.

1 Kings 13:20-22 and 24

NEVER LIVE TO PLEASE MEN

This young prophet had time to reverse the judgment, but that time was limited. It came between his point of departure and his entrance into the house of the deceiving prophet. At any moment during that period, he could have returned home alive. After that, it would be too late. He also had time to repent, from the time he began to saddle his ass for the journey home to the moment he was confronted by the lion.

And did he repent? No one can say for sure. Maybe he did, but that could not change the judgment of God. Clearly he had many opportunities, but in the end, he remain disobedient, having squandered every opportunity.

Beware of False Prophets

Jesus warned us:

Beware of false prophets.   Matthew 7:15

This warning is no less important today than it was in Jesus' time. In fact, it will become more and more important as the days draw to a close and apostasy spreads over the earth.

Psalm 139-140 is a prayer from the heart that we might all pray if we want to remain consistent in God's path and not fall prey to presumptuousness. In this prayer, David cried:

Search me, O God, and know my heart: try me, and know my thoughts: and see if there be any wicked way in me, and lead me in the way everlasting.
                    Psalm 139:23-24

Let God search you today, believe what He tells you, and return back to the path of the will of God by repenting and seeking His forgiveness. Don't wait until it's too late. When Jesus comes, you must be found in good standing with Him. So now is the time to make things right. Beloved, let us concentrate on *Always Being Ready*.

CHAPTER 7

REPENTANCE THAT FAILS TO PRODUCE FORGIVENESS

Then said Saul, I have sinned: return, my son David: for I will no more do thee harm.   1 Samuel 26:21

God is merciful. Therefore, whenever His children pray, they expect to receive anything and everything they ask from Him. But He doesn't always respond as we expect. There are conditions to be met as we approach

God. The power to cancel our debt and our guilt is in the hands of a supernatural God, and the Scriptures show that there are times when men have sought Him for forgiveness, and that forgiveness was not forthcoming. An important example to examine in this regard is the story of King Saul, once the chosen King of Israel and King David, who became Saul's replacement after his untimely death.

TWO MURDERERS, TWO VERY DIFFERENT JUDGMENTS

As we have seen, David committed premeditated murder and was forgiven. Saul was also a murderer. He hated David and attempted on several occasions to kill him. Then he repented (or seemed to repent), but God did not forgive him, and David also felt he could not trust him. In the end, Saul died in his sins, and David took his place as king.

The mistake King Saul made is the same as that made by millions who come to God for forgiveness and find themselves rejected. God judged both men, using the same standard of holiness. He was not judging them based only on what they had done or on what they had said, but on the condition of their hearts—something that only He truly knows.

In God's divine and perfect execution of mercy and judgment, David was forgiven, and King Saul was condemned. Saul was told:

The Strength of Israel will not lie nor repent: for he is not a man, that he should repent.   1 Samuel 15:29

God won't change. We're the ones who have to change. Among the things that He, who judges righteously, hates to see in the heart of man is this:

> *An heart that deviseth wicked imaginations.*
>   Proverbs 6:18

And that was Saul's problem.

REPENTANCE THAT CANNOT BE TRUSTED

When Saul confessed that he had sinned, David could not trust him. The Spirit of God in David's heart would not release him to get anywhere near the king. Saul seemed to be repenting, speaking words that sounded good, but in the process his heart was not fully surrendered to God. In other words, he was lying, and thankfully, God puts within us the spirit of discernment, and so David knew the truth in this situation and refused to reveal himself again to King Saul.

> *The mistake King Saul made is the same as that made by millions who come to God for forgiveness and find themselves rejected!*

David's response in the following chapter shows us that he immediately recognized the presence of deception in the voice of Saul. The Holy Spirit in the life of the believer will either cause us to trust what men say to us or not to trust their words, and He always knows the truth:

> *And David said in his heart, I shall now perish one day by the hand of Saul: there is nothing better for me than that I should speedily escape into the land of the Philistines.* 1 Samuel 27:1

How sad! David decided that he would rather trust in the company of an avowed enemy than in a man of his own nation and race, his king and his father-in-law. Saul could not be trusted.

SAMUEL ALSO DISTRUSTED SAUL

As sad as this was, David was right, and the prophet Samuel came to the same conclusion about Saul. When he asked the king an important question about his failure to obey the command of God, Saul failed to answer honestly. What was God's command to Saul?

> *Now go and smite Amalek, and utterly destroy all that they have, and spare them not; but slay both man and woman, infant and suckling, ox and sheep, camel and ass.* 1 Samuel 15:3

Just think of the carnage that would have been seen

that day, and yet God had to order this slaughter because He is holy and eternally just, and the Amalekites had set their hearts against Him and His people. Saul had a problem with this, and many today also don't understand God and the way He deals with men. Saul made the mistake of deciding to take things into his own hands, and many make the same mistake today.

Here is the question the prophet Samuel would later ask the king:

> *Wherefore then didst thou not obey the voice of the LORD, but didst fly upon the spoil, and didst evil in the sight of the LORD?*　　　　　　　　1 Samuel 15:19

The reason this king could not understand the seriousness of God's command was that he failed to realize that God says what He means. Instead of obeying what God had told him to do, Saul was moved to act on his own philosophy, a humanistic logic, and yield to the people's desires. In other words, he was a king without much spiritual backbone:

> *But the people took of the spoil, sheep and oxen, the chief of the things which should have been utterly destroyed, to sacrifice unto the LORD thy God in Gilgal.*
> 　　　　　　　　1 Samuel 15:21

SAMUEL REBUKED THE KING

Samuel's rebuke and response to King Saul still speak today to men and women who fail to obey God and conclude that He thinks like a man. He doesn't; He never has; and He never will:

> And Samuel said, Hath the LORD as great delight in burnt offerings and sacrifices, as in obeying the voice of the LORD? Behold, to obey is better than sacrifice, and to hearken than the fat of rams.
>
> 1 Samuel 15:22

When we have sinned and displeased God, we must come quickly to Him, repent and seek His forgiveness!

Saul's answer reflected a total lack of honesty on his part, and nothing good ever comes of partial obedience in the things of God. He demands one-hundred-percent obedience:

> And Saul said unto Samuel, Yea, I have obeyed the voice of the LORD, and have gone the way which the LORD sent me.   1 Samuel 15:20

This was clearly not true, and God held it against Saul. We cannot afford to take repentance and forgiveness lightly. Our eternal destiny is dependent upon this divine principle. King Saul dared to toy with the eternal destiny of his soul, and he lost. When we have sinned and displeased God, we must come quickly to Him, repent and seek His forgiveness. This important concept of quickly seeking forgiveness is explored more fully in a later chapter of the book.

DAVID'S APPROACH TO GOD

The Scriptures show us that when we come to God we must have the right attitude. David's attitude was right, and Saul's was wrong. Aside from truthfulness, our attitude must be one of faith and diligence. These are the conditions of the heart that God seeks:

> *But without faith it is impossible to please him; for he that cometh to God must believe that he is, and that he is a rewarder of them that diligently seek him.*
>
> Hebrews 11:6

We are told in the Scriptures that *"a broken and a contrite heart"* the Lord will *"not despise"* (Psalm 51:17). Every penitent heart that has felt the same conviction as David did (after using poor judgment, committing adultery and even ordering premeditated murder) will just as surely be forgiven by the Righteous Judge. David confessed that he hated the crime he had committed against God, who is Holy, and God granted him forgiveness:

> *Have mercy upon me, O God, according to thy loving-kindness: according unto the multitude of thy tender mercies blot out my transgressions. Wash me throughly*

*from mine iniquity, and cleanse me from my sin. For
I acknowledge my transgressions: and my sin is ever
before me.*   Psalm 51:1-3

David went to God in brokenness and humility, and
God did not turn him away.

Saul's Approach to God

The popular philosophy, "I can keep doing this as long
as I don't get caught," is the philosophy of a fool. When a
man or woman takes on this attitude, the heart then becomes hardened through the deceitfulness of riches and
power. Once this pattern sets in, evil actions begin to appear good, and good actions actually begin to appear evil
or foolish. Saul had been chosen from among his brothers
and set over Israel as its first king, but now he was living
recklessly in partial obedience and willful rebellion. His
words seemed to be words of repentance, but they were
not from the heart. There is no partial forgiveness, and so
a partial repentance can never please God or be acceptable to Him.

Why does God seem to be so misunderstood when it
comes to His final word on wrath and judgment? It's because of what Isaiah declared hundreds of years ago, as
we noted in the previous chapter:

*For my thoughts are not your thoughts, neither are your
ways my ways, saith the LORD. For as the heavens are
higher than the earth, so are my ways higher than your
ways, and my thoughts than your thoughts.*
                                                    Isaiah 55:8-9

MAN NEVER KNOWS BETTER THAN GOD

There is a very important fact to consider in these two examples. God expects a man to act like a man and take on the responsibility that He has given him, without reservation and limitation. Obedience at any given moment of our lives must be total, even when what God is telling us doesn't seem to make sense. To King Saul, it didn't make sense to destroy perfectly good animals. Couldn't they be used to sacrifice to God? No, God said, obedience was more important even than sacrifice.

This attitude, that a man knows better than God, has often been seen throughout history. Take the first two sons born into this world: Cain and Abel. The altar of Abel pleased God because it was an altar of obedience and uncompromising sacrifice, but the altar of Cain displeased the Lord because it was all about man's philosophy and reasoning. As a result, the one was blessed and the other was not, and Cain, instead of repenting and receiving forgiveness, was angry about it and killed his brother in a jealous fit of rage. How very sad!

GOD IS ACCUSED OF UNEQUAL FORGIVENESS

Forgiving one murderer and rejecting the other appears to be unequal justice, and today there are many who accuse God and His Word of being unequal when it comes to blessings and judgment. It was true in ancient times as well. The nation of Israel also wanted God to change His ways regarding judgment and blessings. They were, they complained, *"not equal"*:

Yet ye say, The way of the Lord is not equal. Hear now,
O house of Israel; Is not my way equal? are not your
ways unequal?   Ezekiel 18:25

Man was accusing God, because man had failed and God was forced to condemned him. What a contradiction it is when a man has the boldness to point his finger at the Creator and accuse Him of partiality! If it were not for the mercy of a loving God, no man would ever experience salvation. God is infinitely good.

Knowing that fellowship with God is precious and represents the greatest loss anyone could ever experience in life, the truly penitent sinner seeks with all his strength to hold on to that relationship:

And ye shall seek me, and find me, when ye shall
search for me with all your heart.   Jeremiah 29:13

The Spirit of God draws those who seek the gift of repentance and forgiveness. Others turn away in disgust and accuse God of wrongdoing.

OTHER REASONS THAT GOD DOES NOT ANSWER

There may be other reasons that God does not answer a prayer for forgiveness. As noted in the previous chapter, the prophet Samuel cried all night to God, asking for mercy to spare the life of King Saul, but God rejected his prayer. Think about that. God rejected the prayer of a recognized and respected prophet.

Many times before this, Samuel's prayers had been

answered, but not this time. This time, God said no to his request. Why? It was because we cannot repent for the sins of another person, no matter what their relationship to us may be. Parents cannot repent for their children, and pastors cannot repent for their members—even if they repeat the sinners pray, as it is rehearsed to them. Repentance must come from the heart of the sinner himself.

When Samuel kept asking God to forgive Saul, God spoke to Samuel and reminded him that He could never repent or reverse words that He had spoken:

> And the LORD said unto Samuel, How long wilt thou mourn for Saul, seeing I have rejected him from reigning over Israel?
> 1 Samuel 16:1

It has to be one of the saddest days in anyone's life when they come to God and are rejected. Samuel must have felt great sorrow when he saw the man he had anointed to be king over Israel, a man whom he had nurtured as

Knowing that fellowship with God is precious and represents the greatest loss anyone could ever experience in life, the truly penitent sinner seeks ... to hold on to that relationship!

a son, now rejected by God. Like Samuel, we are often tempted to reach out to God over and over again, to see if there might be a change in His decree. No one likes to hear that the answer to their petition is no, when we've been conditioned to hearing yes. But once the word goes forth from the Lord, it is irreversible.

This was not the first time God said no to a prophet. He said no to Moses, and He meant it. He actually stopped Moses from asking again for a reversal of his punishment:

> *I pray thee, let me go over, and see the good land that is beyond Jordan, that goodly mountain, and Lebanon. But the LORD was wroth with me for your sakes, and would not hear me: and the LORD said unto me, Let it suffice thee; speak no more unto me of this matter. Get thee up into the top of Pisgah, and lift up thine eyes westward, and northward, and southward, and eastward, and behold it with thine eyes: for thou shalt not go over this Jordan.* Deuteronomy 3:25-27

God also said no to the apostle Paul, and when God says no it's no, not maybe. No one knows for sure what the problem was that Paul was seeking deliverance from. It could have been most anything:

> *For this thing I besought the Lord thrice, that it might depart from me. And He said unto me, My grace is sufficient for thee: for my strength is made perfect in weakness.* 2 Corinthians 12:8-9

104

Whatever Paul's request to the Lord was, he would not receive it. And when God determines and speaks His final word, there is no way He will change His decree:

There are at least two reasons for God's response. First, everyone who seeks forgiveness from God must do it on his or her own. We must repent of our own sins and not the sins of another. When Daniel offered a prayer for the nation of Israel in the land of bondage, he included himself as one of those who had sinned:

We have sinned, and have committed iniquity, and have done wickedly.   Daniel 9:5

O my God, incline thine ear, and hear; open thine eyes, and behold our desolations, and the city which is called by thy name: for we do not present our supplications before thee for our righteousnesses, but for thy great mercies. O Lord, hear; O Lord, forgive; O Lord, hearken and do; defer not, for thine own sake, O my God: for thy city and thy people are called by thy name.
                                    Daniel 9:18-19

The Scriptures make it clear that if we turn from our wicked ways, God will hear us, and Daniel came to the conclusion that he was among those who had *"done wickedly."* So he was well within the divine principles of prayer when he confessed his own sin and that of the nation.

Another instance in which God may not hear and answer positively is when the repentance has come too late. God has a time frame within which forgiveness will

105

be granted, a certain grace period. Therefore there must be, on our part, a willingness to swiftly obey the conviction of the Holy Spirit. Delayed obedience is the same as disobedience.

There is also no place for repentance and forgiveness once a person, church, race or nation reaches the irreversible state of apostasy. When apostasy sets in, the soul and heart of an individual is beyond the point of restoration.

Only God has the spiritual measuring rod to determine when sin and rebellion has reached this point. Sometimes He will reveal it to His servants, and they will speak it forth. Sadly, no one prophesied to us the coming calamity of the Twin Towers, as prophets of God did in Bible days.

God never sent His prophets to speak in some dark corner. Rather He sent them with boldness to warn the world or a particular nation so that everyone could be a witness to what He was about to do. When the prophets of God spoke in this way, what they said proved to be more accurate than the later records of historians.

What are we waiting for? Let us draw near to God while there is yet time. Beloved, let us concentrate on *Always Being Ready*.

CHAPTER 8

WHAT HINDERS REPENTANCE?

I charge thee therefore before God, and the Lord Jesus Christ, who shall judge the quick and the dead at his appearing and his kingdom; preach the word; be instant in season, out of season; reprove, rebuke, exhort with all longsuffering and doctrine. For the time will come when they will not endure sound doctrine; but after their own lusts shall they heap to themselves teach-

ers, having itching ears; and they shall turn away their ears from the truth, and shall be turned unto fables.

2 Timothy 4:1-4

> **When the spirit of man justifies his position and rejects the godly sorrowing that is necessary for repentance, truth is frustrated!**

What hinders repentance? For starters, presumptuousness and pride work together to blind the eyes of man, frustrating him and keeping him from acknowledging his need to repent and seek God's forgiveness for his sins. As a result, the heart of men and women procrastinate and delay responding to the urgent command to quickly turn and make things right with God. When the spirit of man rejects the constant probing of the Holy Spirit, a hardening of the will takes place. Even many Christians experience this.

Godly Sorrow Is Required

When the spirit of man justifies his position and rejects the godly sorrowing that is necessary for repentance, truth is frustrated, and that kind of pride brings about a spiritual downfall. The result is bitterness and deception. The bitterness is evidenced by the fact that the person is angry and refuses to accept truth. Instead, he or she now stubbornly holds to a position that may well damn their soul to Hell:

Now the Spirit speaketh expressly, that in the latter times some shall depart from the faith, giving heed to seducing spirits, and doctrines of devils.

1 Timothy 4:1

One of the seducing spirits spoken of in this verse is hard at work today. It is said that six out of every ten preachers in the United States are now "hooked" on pornography. How sad is that? It is time for repentance and forgiveness, and we must do that before it is too late.

OUR CHARGE

Paul's *"charge"* to the righteous, now, as never before, is to preach God's Word without reservation and with great boldness. Men must hear it and respond to it or else risk losing their souls.

The condition described in this theme passage is the most dangerous one any Christian (or anyone else, for that matter) could possibly find themselves in. People who think like this are heading toward a state of apostasy, from which there can be no return.

WHERE IS THE LINE?

God is unpredictable in many ways, and one of the unpredictable things about Him is this: no one knows just how much sin He will tolerate before He says, "Enough!"

No one knows exactly how much time any given human being has left to repent and seek God's forgiveness. Still, many people insist on playing Russian Roulette with their souls and, thus, gamble away their eternal destiny. As a result, many will surely miss the Rapture and be left behind with only one way to achieve eternal life—being tortured to death for their faith in Christ.

It is foolish for any Christian to put off living holy until tomorrow, for tomorrow may never come:

Go to now, ye that say, Today or to-morrow we will go into such a city, and continue there a year, and buy and sell, and get gain: whereas ye know not what shall be on the morrow. For what is your life? It is even a vapour, that appeareth for a little time, and then vanisheth away. For that ye ought to say, If the Lord will, we shall live, and do this, or that. James 4:13-15

Those who are bound by evil emotional chains desperately need to be set free so that they can be granted God's gift of repentance and forgiveness. When this battle is complete and victory is assured, then their minds will be free to hate what God hates and love what He loves.

Repentance and forgiveness result in freedom. How can we know when a soul is void of this freedom? We can know because of the presence of condemnation and guilt and the absence of joy and peace. When condemnation goes, freedom and joy rush in. If you have no joy, then, based on simple conditional logic, you have no freedom, and if there is no freedom, then there is no deliverance from condemnation. If condemnation governs the heart and soul, the condition of that man or woman is hope-lessness. There is only one way out. Turn to God with repentance and seek His forgiveness.

THE SIN OF PRIDE IN SODOM

Sodom and Gomorrah are often spoken of in the Bible in a very harsh and negative way. These were the twin cities of sin. Was it possible for God to forgive the sinners who lived there? Many mistakenly believe that the only sins of Sodom and Gomorrah were homosexuality, adultery and fornication, but the Bible shows us that there was much more:

> *As I live, saith the Lord GOD, Sodom thy sister hath not done, she nor her daughters, as thou hast done, thou and thy daughters. Behold, this was the iniquity of thy sister Sodom, pride, fulness of bread, and abundance of idleness was in her and in her daughters, neither did she strengthen the hand of the poor and needy. And they were haughty, and committed abomination before me: therefore I took them away as I saw good.*
>
> Ezekiel 16:48-50

The first sin on this particular list is pride. Where there is pride, it can be easily observed that there is an increase in immorality and sexual wickedness. Every nation that is filled with pride today suffers from unchecked sexual lawlessness and wickedness. This is our modern Sodom, and it is made up of America and all the other apostate Western nations. Unless these nations repent, God will do to them as He did to Sodom and Gomorrah.

A LACK OF COMPASSION FOR THE LESS FORTUNATE

Where there is self-centeredness and pride, people cannot seem to care for the needs of *"the poor."* The reason they cannot is that their own hearts are controlled by greed. They want more and more for themselves, and they care little about others.

I don't know if, in this particular verse, the Bible is speaking of the righteous poor or the wicked poor or both. I don't know if it refers to the poor at home or in neighboring lands. What is clear is that the people of Sodom had a spirit of greed, and the result was that they failed to do what God expected them to do for the poor.

For all those who are blessed, God has a specific plan for their giving, and *"remember the poor"* (Galatians 2:10) is His command to those to whom He has entrusted more than enough for their own needs. Every man must consider the fact that he is responsible to God to give cheerfully:

God loveth a cheerful giver. 2 Corinthians 9:7

A failure to show compassion on the poor was one of the reasons God, in His wrath, destroyed the cities of Sodom and Gomorrah.

Sometimes, even when churches (or nations) give large sums of money to help the needy, it becomes a matter of pride for them. And as long as we refuse to repent of the sin of pride, our money amounts to nothing in the eyes of God. He cannot be bribed.

A HARDENED AND INSENSITIVE SPIRIT

The evil of a hardened and insensitive spirit is the sin of many in the developed nations. They have many resources and, instead of using them to bless others, they heap up even more treasures unto themselves. In many of the rich nations, lots of food is wasted, dumped into the garbage or otherwise destroyed. At the same time, hundreds of thousands of children go hungry in other nations and even starve to death. God's Word says to the insensitive:

> *A failure to show compassion on the poor was one of the reasons God, in His wrath, destroyed the cities of Sodom and Gomorrah!*

> *Then I will turn to those on my left and say, "Away with you, you cursed ones, into the eternal fire prepared for the devil and his demons. For I was hungry and you wouldn't feed me; thirsty, and you wouldn't give me anything to drink."*
>
> Matthew 25:41-42, TLB

One day, there will be a reckoning:

And before him shall be gathered all nations: and he shall separate them one from another, as a shepherd divideth his sheep from the goats. Matthew 25:32

Does God discriminate? The choice is ours, not His. If someone is a sheep in eternity, it means that they left this earth that way. After that fateful day of appointment, no one can be spiritually changed. They will remain what they already are:

Then shall the King say unto them on his right hand, Come, ye blessed of my Father, inherit the kingdom prepared for you from the foundation of the world: for I was an hungered, and ye gave me meat; I was thirsty, and ye gave me drink: I was a stranger, and ye took me in: naked, and ye clothed me: I was sick, and ye visited me: I was in prison, and ye came unto me.

Matthew 25:34-36

GOD HAS GOOD RECORDS

God has good records, and they will bring to light all that we have done in this life. No one will be able to claim that those records are somehow mistaken, and no one will be able to change them. The record is what it is. If you have worked unselfishly for Christ, the record will show that fact. And if not, then what can you expect? Because of this, our work for the Lord must be pure with our only motive being that of pleasing Christ, our Master:

Then shall the righteous answer him, saying, Lord, when saw we thee an hungered, and fed thee? or thirsty, and gave thee drink? When saw we thee a stranger, and took thee in? or naked, and clothed thee? Or when saw we thee sick, or in prison, and came unto thee? Matthew 25:37-39

NOTHING IS HIDDEN FROM GOD

We serve an omnipresent and all-knowing God. Nothing escapes His eyes or ears. He sees what is done in darkness, just as He sees what is done in the light. With Him, the night is just as bright as the day, for Christ is the Light of the World. This is the reason it is important to repent and confess our sins now, because it makes no sense to try to hide anything from God. We may lie to everyone else and even to ourselves, but we cannot fool God. The fate of all liars will be *"the lake of fire"* (Revelation 20:14-15).

Jesus said those who have not ministered to the poor have not ministered to Him:

And the King shall answer and say unto them, Verily I say unto you, Inasmuch as ye have done it unto one of the least of these my brethren, ye have done it unto me. Matthew 25:40

WE ARE ONLY STEWARDS OF HIS GOODS

In that day, there will be no excuse for those who refused to accept the fact that we are stewards of all that

115

God has placed in our care. Part of our stewardship is to distribute to those who are in need and to do it cheerfully and generously:

> *Part*
> *of*
> *our*
> *stewardship*
> *is*
> *to*
> *distribute*
> *to*
> *those*
> *who*
> *are*
> *in*
> *need*
> *and*
> *to*
> *do*
> *it*
> *cheerfully*
> *and*
> *generously!*

Then shall he say also unto them on the left hand, Depart from me, ye cursed, into everlasting fire, prepared for the devil and his angels. For I was an hungered, and ye gave me no meat: I was thirsty, and ye gave me no drink: I was a stranger, and ye took me not in: naked, and ye clothed me not: sick, and in prison, and ye visited me not. Matthew 25:41-43

I believe that Christians should read this chapter often, for it contains the sum total of all that we have done on earth for Christ. As the well-known saying goes, "Only what's done for Christ will last." This means that nothing else will stand and be counted worthy for eternity. All else will be loss:

Then shall he answer them, saying, Verily I say unto you, Inasmuch as ye did it not to one of the least of these, ye did it not to me. And these shall go away into everlasting punishment: but the righteous into life eternal. Matthew 25:45-46

What Will Keep Men and Women Out of Heaven?

What will keep men and women out of Heaven? What did Jesus mean when He said:

And then will I profess unto them, I never knew you: depart from me, ye that work iniquity.

Matthew 7:23

Most have thought that such rejection could come only because a person did not believe in Jesus, failed to take communion or didn't speak in tongues, but there is more to iniquity than meets the eye. What we do for *"these little ones"* we are doing for Christ, and what we fail to do for them, we are failing to do for Him. Every act of kindness, every demonstration of love, should be done in His name. It may be nothing more than giving a cup of cold water, but if the motivating power behind that act is our love and attachment to Jesus, it will be rewarded. Conversely, our failures in this regard cannot but hinder us in God's sight.

Could Nebuchadnezzar Have Relieved the Suffering in His World?

Did Daniel perhaps call upon Nebuchadnezzar to aid in feeding the world's poor? We know that the king had enough power, authority and wealth to initiate such a program. So, too, do many nations of the world today. Nothing is specifically said about this in the Scriptures, but this great king could have done it. If he could not have fed *all* the hungry in his world, at the very least, he could have fed many of them. Why is this important? It is important because when Jesus called upon us to follow Him and fulfill His commandments, He specifically stated that we were to feed, clothe and visit *"these little ones"* who were in need.

How many are we to feed? Well, we can begin with one and then work our way up from there. The key is not how much we do, but doing what God has called us to do in gratitude for who He is and what He has done for us. Because He gave Himself to demonstrate His love, we must now have that same love in our hearts and demonstrate it to the world through our compassion for the poor. Jesus fed the people of His day because He had compassion upon them and felt their pangs of hunger.

What about you? Are you being obedient to God's call on your life? Beloved, let us concentrate on *Always Being Ready*

PART III

THE FORGIVENESS THAT WE MUST EXTEND TO OTHERS

CHAPTER 9

JESUS LEFT US AN EXAMPLE

*Then said Jesus, Father, forgive them; for they know
not what they do.*   Luke 23:34

Our loving heavenly Father extends to us the gift
of repentance and forgiveness and, because He is so
ready and willing to grant us this favor, He then requires that we forgive each other:

Forgive, and ye shall be forgiven.   Luke 6:37

Jesus set the example for us in this regard. He forgave all of His enemies, and He did it before He breathed His last breath on this earth. This was a powerful demonstration of Calvary's love.

JESUS HAD TO DIE

It may seem contradictory to some for Jesus to forgive those who killed Him because He had to die for the sins of mankind, and the Father had preordained before the foundations of the world that He would die at the hands of men. Still, Jesus forgave those who were used to accomplish it.

But was the forgiveness Jesus spoke of on the cross only for those who were instrumental in His death? Was it for all those who had gathered there at Calvary to witness His punishment? Or was it for all who would be saved? Some have speculated that this was even forgiveness for the whole world and for every generation. Who can know for sure? Only the Lord. But one thing is certain: these words, spoken by Jesus, cannot be construed to mean that anyone and everyone can have eternal life without doing what He has taught must be done to find it. Even Mary, Jesus' earthly mother, could only be saved through believing and obeying the Gospel and accepting the finished work of Christ on the cross:

Therefore let all the house of Israel know assuredly, that God hath made that same Jesus, whom ye have

122

crucified, both Lord and Christ. Now when they heard this, they were pricked in their heart, and said unto Peter and to the rest of the apostles, Men and brethren, what shall we do? Then Peter said unto them, Repent, and be baptized every one of you in the name of Jesus Christ for the remission of sins, and ye shall receive the gift of the Holy Ghost. Acts 2:36-38

Whatever men do in this life that is against God's commandments, they are responsible for it, and they must repent and receive forgiveness.

FORGIVENESS IS NOT AUTOMATIC

Some say that in that moment Jesus was forgiving the whole world because He died for all humanity, but regardless of what men might say, we know that truth is not the same as popular philosophy. The Word of God declares:

And ye shall know the truth, and the truth shall make you free.
John 8:32

These words, spoken by Jesus, cannot be construed to mean that anyone and everyone can have eternal life without doing what He has taught must be done to find it!

123

Unless men and women repent and believe the Gospel they cannot enter into the Kingdom of Heaven. The same Jesus who prayed *"Father, forgive them,"* also said:

> *The time is fulfilled, and the kingdom of God is at hand: repent ye, and believe the gospel.*   Mark 1:15

Peter wrote to the early Church:

> *Forasmuch as ye know that ye were not redeemed with corruptible things, as silver and gold, from your vain conversation received by tradition from your fathers; but with the precious blood of Christ, as of a lamb without blemish and without spot: who verily was foreordained before the foundation of the world, but was manifest in these last times for you.*   1 Peter 1:18-20

Those who were directly responsible for the death of Jesus on that day were ordained by God, because Jesus had to die. He must become the sacrificial Lamb, given for the sins of all mankind. For this very purpose, He offered Himself up willingly, but men had to be involved to shed His blood that day, and He forgave them.

THE LONG-AWAITED MOMENT

This moment in time had long before been prophesied:

> *And I will put enmity between thee and the woman, and between thy seed and her seed; it shall bruise thy head, and thou shalt bruise his heel.*   Genesis 3:15

Now, thousands of years later, these particular men were given the assignment, and it must be done God's way. His way, as it turned out, was for Jesus to face death on the cross. So, in carrying out this long-appointed sentence upon Jesus, these men were actually fulfilling the promise of the Father. The death of the Lamb was necessary so that the plan of God could be fulfilled:

For of a truth against thy holy child Jesus, whom thou hast anointed, both Herod, and Pontius Pilate, with the Gentiles, and the people of Israel, were gathered together, for to do whatsoever thy hand and thy counsel determined before to be done.　　　Acts 4:27-28

This passage clearly shows us that what happened that day was by predetermination of the counsel of God. These men had to do what God had preordained, and they were forgiven for it. But that was not their passport into eternal life. They would still be condemned if they failed to believe and obey the Gospel.

Did they believe? Not much time had passed before those who heard these words, *"Father, forgive them,"* would hear the Gospel preached and, sadly, the majority of them would refuse to believe it and, in this way, they brought condemnation upon themselves:

And they called them, and commanded them not to speak at all nor teach in the name of Jesus. Acts 4:18

How foolish of these learned leaders, for, in reality, every man is a servant of God, whether he knows it or not and whether he likes it or not.

MAN IS THE SERVANT OF GOD, WILLINGLY OR OTHERWISE

Even the pagan King Nebuchadnezzar was God's servant. His armies captured the children of Israel and took them into bondage in Babylon, to satisfy God's wrath and as a punishment for their disobedience. Nebuchadnezzar was not punished for taking God's people captive. God had ordained him for that very purpose:

> *Nebuchadnezzar was not punished for taking God's people captive. God had ordained him for that very purpose!*

And now have I given all these lands into the hand of Nebuchadnezzar the king of Babylon, my servant; and the beasts of the field have I given him also to serve him.
Jeremiah 27:6

The king did not have to repent for this service he rendered to God. Later, however, when he committed iniquity in the land, God sent Daniel to let him know that he would have to repent, and he did (after seven years of humiliation). God is just, and He did not punish Nebuchadnezzar for the things he was under orders, as a servant, to do.

How can we say that those who killed Jesus had to do it? If they had not crucified Him, we could not and would not be saved today. Still, Jesus forgave them, and He did it as an example for us. Now we are faced with the humble task of forgiving those who have done us evil, and we must do it while we have time. This act of forgiving will free the soul and spirit for fellowship with God and will also express to the whole world the love Jesus preached when He commanded us to love our enemies:

> *But I say unto you, Love your enemies, bless them that curse you, do good to them that hate you, and pray for them which despitefully use you, and persecute you; that ye may be the children of your Father which is in heaven.* Matthew 5:44-45

The words of forgiveness uttered by Jesus had to be offered before He gave up His spirit. There on the cross, He must demonstrate to everyone the principles He had taught in life. He was the Master Teacher, and He must remain Master of the circumstances of His death for the benefit of all concerned.

So there on the cross, Jesus set this example that we must now follow. Each of us must forgive those who have done us evil, and it must be done before we leave this earth. This is our responsibility as Christians. If even Jesus had to do it, how much more do we have to do the same?

SEARCH YOUR MEMORY

At times, we may have to search the inventory of our hearts and minds, mulling over in our minds the many conflicts life has brought our way, and taking whatever necessary action to insure that we can look any man or woman in the face and harbor no ill feelings against them. Instead of seeing them as enemies, we must look at them as brothers and sisters. If they don't happen to be part of the family of God, that doesn't lessen our responsibility in this regard. The same forgiveness is required. This is not about the people involved; it's all about Jesus. Our objective must always be to be more like Him:

> *Let this mind be in you, which was also in Christ Jesus: ...*
> *And being found in fashion as a man, he humbled himself, and became obedient unto death, even the death of the cross. Wherefore God also hath highly exalted him, and given him a name which is above every name.*
> Philippians 2:5 and 8-9

Humility destroys pride, and whether the men and women who have wronged us repent or not, it is still our responsibility to forgive them. Let us do as Jesus did on the cross. He did not delay. He was about to "give up the ghost" and, before He left this world, He must demonstrate the power of agape love, one of the important lessons He had taught during His time on earth. Jesus is our merciful High Priest. Let us follow His example.

UNFORGIVENESS IMPEDES THE PRESENCE OF GOD

The Holy Spirit cannot abide in our lives if we have an unforgiving heart. Therefore we can boldly say that there are two important principles when it comes to forgiveness: First, God forgives us, and then, we must forgive others. These two commands are inseparable and cannot function independently of each other. One cannot exist without the other. It is impossible to be blessed with God's forgiveness, if the heart is unforgiving toward others. Jesus said very clearly:

> *For if ye forgive men their trespasses, your heavenly Father will also forgive you: but if ye forgive not men their trespasses, neither will your Father forgive your trespasses.* Matthew 6:14-15

How are you doing in this regard? Have you forgiven those who have wronged you? Don't delay another day.

PRACTICING FORGIVENESS

As forgiven creatures, God calls on us to practice forgiveness toward others. Our Lord Jesus Christ, in fact, has commanded us to forgive a person seventy times seven (or four hundred and ninety) times. If Jesus calls upon us, as mere men, to forgive our fellowman four hundred and ninety times, that must mean that He has forgiven us at least that many times:

> *Then came Peter to him, and said, Lord, how oft shall my brother sin against me, and I forgive him? till seven times? Jesus saith unto him, I say not unto thee, Until seven times: but, Until seventy times seven.* Matthew 18:21-22

Being willing to forgive again and again is a clear indication that we are practicing a spiritual truth. It quickly becomes a habit of forgiveness, part of our new character. This is not a pharisaical demand, just a manifestation of Gospel obedience. Just as we are convicted to speak the truth to develop a character of honesty, so too this love to forgive helps to mature the new nature of Christ in us.

BUT CAN I FORGIVE AND FORGET?

Forgetting is not always easy, for God has blessed us with the ability to remember. That's why we often find ourselves unable to forget wrongs—no matter how hard we try. Sometimes it seems that it's easier to remember than to forget. Thank God He will never give us a test without providing a way of escape. God's divine plan will always work.

The spiritual solution that can deliver the mind from the agony of the pains of remembering what we would like to forget is in the Word of God:

For the word of God is quick, and powerful, and sharper than any two-edged sword, piercing even to the dividing asunder of soul and spirit, and of the joints and marrow, and is a discerner of the thoughts and intents of the heart. Hebrews 4:12

The secret of forgetting wrongdoing is to starve the memory. In other words, refuse to feed those thoughts. Use the spiritual weapons of the Word of God and literally speak to your mind audibly. This has proven to be the most effective means to gaining deliverance from this sort of mental attack. It has been said that the most powerful way to destroy a thought is by applying the spoken Word of God to it:

> *(For the weapons of our warfare are not carnal, but mighty through God to the pulling down of strong holds;) casting down imaginations, and every high thing that exalteth itself against the knowledge of God, and bringing into captivity every thought to the obedience of Christ.* 2 Corinthians 10:4-5

Thoughts are imaginations that can be fed, so don't feed them, and they will die. Some people have used the medium of singing effectively in this regard, and there are many other spiritual weapons available to the believer. It's time to get serious about forgiving others. Beloved, let us concentrate on *Always Being Ready.*

Chapter 10

Joseph as a Type of Christ

And Joseph said unto them, Fear not: for am I in the place of God? But as for you, ye thought evil against me; but God meant it unto good, to bring to pass, as it is this day, to save much people alive. Now therefore fear ye not: I will nourish you, and your little ones. And he comforted them, and spake kindly unto them.

Genesis 50:19-21

Forgiveness is not an option—either with God or with us. Just as God never fails to forgive when we truly repent and turn to Him, He also taught forgiveness as a responsibility and command to every believer in the Body of Christ.

FORGIVENESS CLEARS THE WAY FOR BLESSING

Forgiveness clears the way for blessing. For example, when we present our offerings to God, we must do so with a clean heart, one free of unforgiveness. Jesus said:

Therefore if thou bring thy gift to the altar, and there rememberst that thy brother hath aught against thee; leave there thy gift before the altar, and go thy way; first be reconciled to thy brother, and then come and offer thy gift.
Matthew 5:23-24

Our forgiveness of others, then, is the passport which authorizes us to enter into communion with God and to become a recipient of the blessings His fellowship affords.

Our forgiveness of others, then, is the passport which authorizes us to enter into communion with God and to become a recipient of the blessings His fellowship affords!

We cannot be accepted into the presence of God until we have made everything right in this regard. Forgiving others clears the pathway for our prayers to be answered. The reason, then, that so many prayers go unanswered is that there exists the presence of an unforgiving spirit. In order for God to bless us, our hearts must be pure, and they cannot be pure when they are filled with unforgiveness.

These are important truths taught by our Lord Jesus Christ. We must be forgiven to enter the Kingdom of Heaven, and we must forgive one another if we expect to be together throughout eternity. Once God has forgiven us, He then calls upon us to forgive each other. The Old Testament story of Joseph is particularly beautiful in this regard, and it is because Joseph was a type of Christ.

JOSEPH FORGAVE HIS BROTHERS

Joseph's story is found in the book of Genesis. There we learn that his older brothers hated him, were jealous of him and conspired against him to do him great harm. One of the most wonderful things we notice in this narrative is the amazing fact that Joseph continued to love his brothers, even when he knew that they had sold him into slavery and then had given their father falsified evidence to suggest that he had been killed by some wild beast. This shows that Joseph had a pure heart toward God, and because of that, hatred for his brothers could not find a permanent dwelling place there.

Because of the purity of Joseph's heart, God exercised His foreknowledge and blessed the lad many years before he was able to actually tell his brothers that he forgave them. Jesus said of a heart like Joseph's:

Blessed are the pure in heart: for they shall see God.
                                          Matthew 5:8

BECOMING THE JOSEPH IN YOUR FAMILY

It's a wonderful blessing to become the Joseph of your family. Those who are blessed with this gift have a heart that is pure, but they are also blessed with possessions and the generosity of heart to share those possessions with their siblings. The Josephs among us always find favor with both God and man.

When we forgive others, we are standing in God's place, as His servants, to do what He would do and what He wants us to do, expressing to others His grace and compassion. Joseph was able to recognize, thousands of years ahead of his time, a New Testament truth:

And we know that all things work together for good to them that love God.   Romans 8:28

When Joseph's brothers were finally able to ask his forgiveness for what they had done, their words and actions also represented the manifestation of a genuine spirit of repentance. There were times when they realized that, punishment for crimes such as theirs being so great, they should have become his slaves for life:

And his brethren also went and fell down before his face; and they said, Behold, we be thy servants.
                                                    Genesis 50:18

Interestingly enough, Joseph actually had the power to enslave or imprison his brothers for life. But, again, he was a type of Christ, and as such he chose to forgive those who had conspired to do him such devastating harm. How great is the love of our God toward each of us!

JOSEPH UNDERSTOOD THE PRINCIPLES OF CHRIST BEFORE HIS TIME

Before he died, Jacob, Joseph's father, left him a charge, that he should forgive his brothers for their sins against him. Joseph had already done this in his heart, but the time eventually came when he was able to verbally express words of kindness to his brothers.

Hundreds of years later, the apostle Paul, under the inspiration of the Holy Spirit, spoke these words about forgiveness among believers:

And be ye kind one to another, tenderhearted, forgiving one another, even as God for Christ's sake hath forgiven you.   Ephesians 4:32

Such forgiveness was the motivation for the great demonstration of Christ's love displayed on the cross of Calvary. Hanging there in unspeakable agony, He was able to pray those amazing words: *"Father, forgive them; for they know not what they do"* (Luke 23:34). When Jesus

spoke those words, He was setting forth an example of
the love He had taught His disciples:

> *But I say unto you which hear, Love your enemies, do*
> *good to them which hate you, bless them that curse you,*
> *and pray for them which despitefully use you.*
>
> Luke 6:27-28

He promised wonderful joy and blessing to those who
obeyed this godly practice of forgiveness from the heart:

> *But love ye your enemies, and do good, and lend, hop-*
> *ing for nothing again; and your reward shall be great,*
> *and ye shall be the children of the Highest; for he is*
> *kind unto the unthankful and to the evil.*   Luke 6:35

Forgiveness is the purest expression of God's love to
mankind, and it is the same when we exercise it toward
our fellow men and women. When genuine forgiveness is
present, power is created through love and we can then
have joy and peace of mind. Without divine forgiveness,
there is nothing in the heart of man but untold misery
and hopelessness. Why do so many people choose bondage with the prince of darkness when the Prince of Peace
welcomes them with open arms?

Wouldn't you like to be a Joseph to your generation?
Beloved, let us concentrate on *Always Being Ready.*

CHAPTER 11

DON'T WAIT UNTIL IT'S TOO LATE TO FORGIVE

And that, knowing the time, that now it is high time to awake out of sleep: for now is our salvation nearer than when we believed. The night is far spent, the day is at hand: let us therefore cast off the works of darkness, and let us put on the armour of light.

Romans 13:11-12

It is impossible to forgive someone for the wrongs they have done to us or to receive forgiveness from them for something we have done to offend or hurt them once they have already left this life. As long as such a person is living, there is hope of forgiveness and freedom from guilt, but we must take action while there is time to do so. Once they have died, that's it. It's too late.

We must be on time with our messages of repentance and forgiveness, if our goal is to live each day in a state of joyful expectation of the promise of eternal life. Sadly, too often we are caught procrastinating, and our message of repentance and forgiveness is delivered too late. It happened to a friend of mine.

DELIVERING AN IMPORTANT MESSAGE

I was leaving for a trip to my native Trinidad, and this friend asked if I would mind carrying a message to his father, who was gravely ill. He wanted to let his father know that he had forgiven him for what he had done to his mother, and he was sorry that he had held so much hatred and bitterness against his father through the years. He had prepared a letter expressing this, and his hope was that it would bring reconciliation between him and his father. I agreed to deliver the letter upon my arrival in the island.

I had visited his father on an earlier trip, to inform him, on behalf of his son, that the son was alive and living in New York. For many years the father had believed that his son was dead, and he was happy to hear that it was not so. I had also taken a few photographs to the father, so that he could see what his son looked like now that he was thirty. There were tears in his eyes as he looked them over, and he was very grateful for my visit.

This Was to Be the Day

Now, this was to be the day to finally put an end to all the bitterness of the past, to finally put to rest the long-held animosities between father and son. I got a taxi to take me to the man's home, and I was excited. I couldn't wait to see the joy on this man's face as he was released from so much pent-up emotional pain. Now, at last, the past could be forgotten, and both father and son could concentrate on living their tomorrows. I was about to be terribly disappointed.

The driver of the taxi I hailed that day was a friend from school days, and as we talked, I asked about the man I was on my way to visit. His answer stunned me. The man had already died. There was no one to visit, and the well-intentioned letter I carried had come too late. There was no one to receive it or appreciate its importance. I was deeply saddened for my friend. Both he and his father had been robbed

> *Too often we are caught procrastinating, and our message of repentance and forgiveness is delivered too late!*

of peace and joy because he delayed too long in doing what he knew had to be done. Now he would have to live with this the rest of his life.

As this book goes to press, some years have passed, and both father and son have left this world. That frees me to tell their sad story. Please don't let it be your story too.

No Forgiveness After Death

We all know that there is no forgiveness after death, just as there is no forgiveness after a state of apostasy has engulfed a nation or a people:

> *And as it is appointed unto men once to die, but after this the judgment: so Christ was once offered to bear the sins of many; and unto them that look for him shall he appear the second time without sin unto salvation.* Hebrews 9:27-28

For the child of God, the Great Judgment will not be a time of sadness or regret, but a time of jubilation. We can say, as Paul, that *"to live is Christ, and to die is gain"* (Philippians 1:21). To gain that hope we must repent before the Rapture, and then remain *"instant in season"* and *"out of season"* (2 Timothy 4:2). And to live in freedom of spirit in the presence of God, we must willingly and quickly forgive one another of all wrongs. If Jesus could forgive those who tortured and murdered Him, you can forgive those who have wronged you too. Do it now, before it's too late.

Even Paul Sought Reconciliation

Are you somehow too good for repentance, too good to seek reconciliation? Consider the fact that even the apostle Paul repented in this regard:

> *And Barnabas determined to take with them John, whose surname was Mark. But Paul thought not good to take him with them, who departed from them from Pamphylia, and went not with them to the work. And the contention was so sharp between them, that they departed asunder one from the other: and so Barnabas took Mark, and sailed unto Cyprus; and Paul chose Silas, and departed, being recommended by the brethren unto the grace of God.* Acts 15:37-40

The restoration and reunion that later took place between the apostle Paul and the much younger disciple John Mark confirms to us that, on this side of Heaven, the child of God must always be ready to repent and seek forgiveness and reconciliation. Before we can believe that we are entitled to a place among holy men and women, we have to do as Jesus did just before He died on Calvary. He forgave all—even his enemies.

A Misunderstanding?

Paul and Mark had what some might call a misunderstanding, but the result of it was violent separation, and this even affected Paul's relationship to a former trusted companion—Barnabas. But God is merciful, and

143

> *Paul later expressed a personal desire to be reconciled with the younger man. Such restoration results in the differences being removed and believers becoming one again in fellowship.*

He brought Paul and John Mark to face each other again, so that there would be *"no schism in the body"* (1 Corinthians 12:25).

Could this rift between Paul and John Mark possibly have been caused by spiritual pride? Whatever it may have been, we know that God's love for these two men caused them to meet again here on earth and be reconciled. Waiting to do it in Heaven would have been too late. These things must be done here. It cannot be done once we leave this world:

For Demas hath forsaken me, having loved this present world, and is departed unto Thessalonica; Crescens to Galatia, Titus unto Dalmatia. Only Luke is with me. Take Mark, and bring him with thee: for he is profitable to me for the ministry. 2 Timothy 4:10-11

PAUL WAS WRONG

Mark had been rejected by Paul, and so their restoration to fellowship required that Paul come to the realization that he had demonstrated an unforgiving spirit toward Mark and his youthfulness. Paul later expressed a personal desire to be reconciled with the younger man. Such restoration results in the differences being removed and believers becoming one again in fellowship.

Paul saw the need for Mark, and Mark understood the reason there had been a breakdown of relationship. Mark was in a position to forgive Paul, once he understood that Paul's present attitude came from the heart of a man who now understood his mistake.

Some young Christians seem to have a wealth of patience. Is it because they have more time to make sure that things are not done in a spirit of haste?

Whatever the case, there must be in us a demonstration of the love which Jesus taught and modeled. Paul, in writing to the Galatian church, mentioned this type of love as the very first among the fruits of the Spirit (see Galatians 5:22). Love, of course, is followed in the list by others: *"joy, peace, gentleness and meekness."* These were all lacking in the angry encounter that Paul had earlier with John Mark.

What an important job Barnabas had! He had to share with Mark the truths of the power of the Holy Spirit and try to keep him from having a wrong concept of the apostle Paul, a man who greatly demonstrated the gifts of the Holy Spirit but who seemed to lack the fruit of the Spirit on this particular occasion. Paul's outburst of anger must have caught John Mark off-guard, and it's no different today, as young Christians observe the conduct of older, supposedly more mature, believers and must learn to deal with their "personality quirks."

May God help us to realize that we are all frail human creatures and may we be able to show kindness and understanding to each other—regardless of our past failures. And, most importantly, may we not wait too long to do it. Tomorrow may be too late. Beloved, let us concentrate on *Always Being Ready*.

CHAPTER 12

A FORGIVING CHURCH

But go ye and learn what that meaneth, I will have mercy, and not sacrifice: for I am not come to call the righteous, but sinners to repentance.

Matthew 9:13

There is such a stark contrast between a forgiving and an unforgiving church.

A FORGIVING CHURCH

> *The testimonies of many in that congregation were based on this demonstration of love that made the church a true place of fellowship!*

I will always remember my visits to a forgiving church. I had the privilege of speaking there on several occasions. As I entered the sanctuary, there was a strong witness of the joy and peace of the Lord. The church was far from perfect, but genuine Christian love, compassion and joy in the Holy Spirit could be felt the moment I entered it.

I vividly recall being greeted on one occasion with a broad smile on the face of an usher that reflected such joy that it made an impact on me I doubt that I will ever forget. The odd thing was that I was there that day to share in the needed comfort and support for the church on the event of the loss of its pastor, a good friend of mine.

The testimonies of many in that congregation were based on this demonstration of love that made the church a true place of fellowship. Visitors who were on drugs or had other sinful habits were warmly received and then ministered to. They heard the truth, graciously presented to them with wisdom and love, and they felt the Holy Spirit at work in that place.

Those who testified at that particular meeting spoke about the church's willingness to forgive. When they had first come to the church, help was immediately offered to them. They could sense that they would not be condemned in that place because of their dependence on drugs. Instead, someone let them know that their hope was in trusting Christ. They felt the spirit of forgiveness and, within a very short time, came to believe that they could indeed be helped in that place.

Not all of them changed overnight. Some of them visited again and again, and sometimes they returned no better than they had been when they last attended. Still, because of the constant prayer going up in that place and the consistent effort being made for evangelism, they sensed that God was working through the church to save and deliver them. Finally, after many months or sometimes even years of procrastination and flip-flopping, they were able to allow the Holy Spirit to take control of their lives and deliver them from the jaws of the evil one. This was the testimony of a forgiving church.

A FORGIVING CHURCH HAS DETERMINATION

A forgiving church has the determination to believe God for the impossible. There is hope there for mothers and fathers that their children will one day be delivered from all the demonic forces controlling their lives in this untoward generation.

Today, many are looking desperately for such a

church. Men and women in every city run from church to church, looking (often in vain), for an assembly in which the shepherd has been set in the place as overseer by the Holy Ghost and has a forgiving heart.

The Pastor of a Forgiving Church

King David was once a shepherd himself, and in that position, he labored to save the flock from the wolves, bears and lions that were drawn to attack the defenseless creatures under his care. Although just a lad, he would kill such predators or drive them away. He was not about to abandon the flock or allow any harm to come to them. And he never blamed the sheep for getting into trouble. Instead, he set his heart to deliver them:

> *And David said unto Saul, Thy servant kept his father's sheep, and there came a lion, and a bear, and took a lamb out of the flock: and I went out after him, and smote him, and delivered it out of his mouth: and when he arose against me, I caught him by his beard, and smote him, and slew him. Thy servant slew both the lion and the bear: and this uncircumcised philistine shall be as one of them, seeing he hath defied the armies of the living God.* 1 Samuel 17:34-36

The pastor of a forgiving church places the good of the sheep above all else, understanding that he is responsible to God for their safety. Sadly, today we often find that the opposite is true. Many of those who call themselves pastors actually feed on the flock and abandon them when any sign of trouble comes. Rather than laboring to feed and protect the flock, they become fat by using the flock of God for merchandise. This clearly is not pleasing to our Father God. Every pastor should be a man with spiritual integrity.

Paul wrote to the early Church:

That we henceforth be no more children, tossed to and fro, and carried about with every wind of doctrine, by the sleight of men, and cunning craftiness, whereby they lie in wait to deceive: but speaking the truth in love, may grow up into him in all things, which is the head, even Christ. Ephesians 4:14-15

God's men must be strong in the ministry of the Word in order to skillfully speak against the craftiness of those who come in with questions to derail the truth. He must defend the righteousness required of everyone who is seeking deliverance from sinful habits. Wisdom and divine intelligence are necessary if he is to offer salvation.

Many of our modern churches are very sophisticated and proper in their organization, and there's nothing wrong with a church building being well constructed, with marble floors, well-kept bathrooms and professional music. God is honored with cleanliness and order, so all of these things have their place in the ministry. But if a church has all of this and still there is no room to welcome sinners to find hope and forgiveness to save their dying soul, such a church has lost its purpose and mission in this world.

Every visitor to any Christian church should be

overwhelmed with a desire to return to another Gospel meeting, and this is always the case in a forgiving church. Churches such as these seem to have a spiritual magnet that draws men and women, just as crowds followed Jesus everywhere He went. They even went into the desert to hear Him speak of the Kingdom of God. Wherever the Man from Galilee went, people came from all directions with a desire to hear more and more. And so it should be with us.

An Open Door

The Church of the Lord Jesus Christ must have an open door policy in which anyone and everyone is welcomed and treated equally. The rich and educated must not be allowed to feel that there is a special seat for them in God's House. Jesus showed no favoritism among those who sought Him.

Jesus also had no fear of those who chose to follow Him. Today there seems to be far too much fear in the church, and congregations commonly embrace one group of people but not another. They are actually cold toward those who don't seem to fit their "profile." But religious profiling, just like racial profiling, is not of God, and a forgiving church cannot allow this type of spirit to enter or control its sanctuary.

The power that reaches out to men and women from a forgiving church is the work of the Holy Spirit. This explains why religion has no power to bring hope to the world. A forgiving church is consumed with promoting

Christ and with preaching the whole counsel of God. It will faithfully present Calvary's love and God's justice through the Holy Spirit.

GOD HAS CHARGED PASTORS

As we noted in an earlier chapter, God has charged pastors, shepherds of His flock, to remember that they are accountable to Him, to feed His Church. Paul declared to the Ephesian elders:

Wherefore I take you to record this day, that I am pure from the blood of all men. For I have not shunned to declare unto you all the counsel of God. Take heed therefore unto yourselves, and to all the flock, over the which the Holy Ghost hath made you overseers, to feed the church of God, which he hath purchased with his own blood.

Acts 20:26-28

There seems to be far too much fear in the church, and congregations commonly embrace one group of people but not another!

Then he said something startling:

For I know this, that after my departing shall grievous wolves enter in among you, not sparing the flock.

Acts 20:29

This was a very prophetic statement, and it is still being fulfilled today. This phenomenon has continued from the time of the ministry of the apostle Paul, but now, in our time, it seems to have accelerated at an alarming rate.

A forgiving church never allows wolves to prey on the flock. Rather, the care of the flock is the chief concern of its leaders. Those whom the Holy Ghost has not ordained to be shepherds over the flock cannot seem to help themselves, and they become wolves and hirelings. They care nothing for the flock, only for their own welfare. In a forgiving church, gracious and loving shepherds care for the sheep, because they were ordained by the Holy Ghost to be overseers according to the will of God.

THE CHURCH IS NOT A COLLECTION AGENCY

A forgiving church is not some religious collection agency. It has a passion for missions and a burden for the lost. Its leaders are always on the lookout for a hungry and thirsty person to come through their doors, and they are only too eager and willing to help that person find new life in Christ and escape the world of evil and wickedness. There is no tendency on their part to look at a visitor as an addition to their list of tithing members. Rather, they see every newcomer as a wonderful opportunity to share the love of Jesus through the Gospel, and they feel a responsibility to each one, to warn them of the wages of sin and welcome them into the family of God.

In contrast, much of the preaching and other programs going on in our churches today is little more than empty religious noise. Paul warned the Corinthians:

Though I speak with the tongues of men and of angels, and have not charity, I am become as sounding brass, or a tinkling cymbal. 1 Corinthians 13:1

In the Church, there must be an absence of pride, a true demonstration of God's love and the spirit of forgiveness. Such a church, at times, may not have much to offer, but what it does have is delivered with love and compassion. And that's what it takes to get the job done.

An Unforgiving Church

An unforgiving church has no testimony of deliverance. Like the church of Laodicea, it has lost its first love. The charitable giving and religious works it offers to gain righteousness are rejected by God. He said:

Because thou sayest, I am rich, and increased with goods, and have need of nothing; and knowest not that thou art wretched, and miserable, and poor, and blind, and naked ... Revelation 3:17

God knows the condition of the unforgiving church, and He also knows how and why it got into that spiritual condition and how it can be delivered. We are warned in the Scriptures of the deceitfulness of riches, and we cannot help but notice that people are very commonly deceived as their riches increase. Therefore we are told not to set our hearts on wealth and to be careful, as we possess more and more of it, not to allow it to affect our hearts. This is true for churches, as well as individuals.

> *Because the Holy Ghost is the Chief Administrator of the Church, no one comes in and out without receiving from Him joy and a divine purpose for living!*

God, in His mercy, sent a message to the angel of the church in Laodicea, expressing His love and calling that church to repent and return to Him:

As many as I love, I rebuke and chasten: be zealous therefore, and repent. Revelation 3:19

THE SPIRIT OF AN UNFORGIVING CHURCH

The unforgiving church is like a poisonous cobra. If you get too close, within its circumference of influence or striking distance, you may be caught in its deadly embrace. Run from that place as fast as you can. If you stay there too long, beyond the grace period, you will be in immediate danger of receiving what could be a lethal dose of poison. Even if you survive such an event, you will be scarred for life.

Of course, I'm referring to emotional and spiritual pains, but these can hurt more than a migraine headache. They're so painful that only the power of the Holy Spirit can heal you from them. And the memories of it all will remain with you for years. Beware, lest the venom of the unforgiving church poison you for the rest of your life. This is an important word of caution. Leave that Hellhole before it damages you forever.

Chief Administrator

Because the Holy Ghost is the Chief Administrator of the Church, no one comes in and out without receiving from Him joy and a divine purpose for living. The manifestation of the power of joy and love can lift us to a spiritual level of hope and a closer attachment to Christ. The unforgiving church lacks these things and cannot deliver anyone who seeks to be free from the bondage of hopelessness and loneliness.

The unforgiving church is famous for kicking out onto the street those they deem undesirable. In this regard, the established church is often worse than ungodly corporations. Too often, members, who have been paying tithes and giving offerings for many years, supporting all the church events and helping out with every moneyraising program to maintain the leadership in high style (I call them fatcats), are forgotten in their senior years and neglected in their nursing homes. These members, who were used as merchandise in the business called the church, are now out of sight and out of mind.

I'm not saying that this is the case with all churches, but sadly it is the attitude of many, especially the megachurches. To some, this may sound too gloomy to mention, but it is, after all, what Jesus prophesied would come to pass during the end of the Church Age:

And many false prophets shall rise, and shall deceive
many. And because iniquity shall abound, the love of
many shall wax cold.   Matthew 24:11-12

In all of this, there is reason to rejoice. Jesus said that when we see these things, we should rejoice, for our re-demption is drawing near. We should not be deceived and fall prey to these temptations. We are safe, as long as we remain in a spiritual state of repentance, forgiveness and cleansing, and as long as we are walking worthy of our holy calling in Christ Jesus and keeping true to His Word, and as long as we forgive as He has forgiven us. Unfortu-nately, that is not the case with many.

HAVE WE FORGOTTEN?

Have we forgotten that Christ is coming back for a glorious Church, without spot or wrinkle:

That he might present it to himself a glorious church,
not having spot, or wrinkle, or any such thing; but that
it should be holy and without blemish.
                                        Ephesians 5:27

The Church which is waiting for the Lord to come in the Rapture is a glorious Church. So why do people continue to attend ungodly and unforgiving churches, knowing that what is done there will only vex their righteous souls from day to day? How do they bear all the foolishness and gimmickry and fundraising schemes? The Bible has a word for those who are not being fed in their churches and have no caring shepherd to help prepare them for that which is to come:

> *Wherefore come out from among them, and be ye separate, saith the Lord, and touch not the unclean thing; and I will receive you. And will be a Father unto you, and ye shall be my sons and daughters, saith the Lord Almighty.*   2 Corinthians 6:17-18

Don't let the Rapture take place while you are still sitting in an unforgiving church. Get serious about your soul and don't risk its welfare for social gain. Beloved, let us concentrate on *Always Being Ready*.

PART IV

ARE YOU READY?

CHAPTER 13

AN UNREPENTANT NATION CANNOT PROSPER

*What do ye imagine against the L*ORD*? he will make an utter end; affliction shall not rise up the second time.*

Nahum 1:9

The events of 9-11 should not have been a surprise to the saints of God who know that He is the same yesterday, today and forever, that He always brings judgment based upon His holiness, and that He *"is angry with the wicked every day"* (Psalm 7:11). God spoke strongly to us through the events of 9-11, but the nation failed to listen. He spoke again through the devastation of Hurricane Katrina, but still the nation refused to hear. It was no surprise then, when the financial meltdown occurred, that there was no call for national repentance from our churches. Clearly we have become hardened and at ease as a nation.

NAHUM'S QUESTION DEMANDS AN ANSWER

Nahum the prophet asked this important question, and we must ask a similar question today. Will this nation, once known around the world as a nation under God, but which has lost its reverential fear of the Almighty, ever rise again unless there is repentance? And is there yet time for America to repent and be offered forgiveness? Or are we, perhaps, already in an irrevocable state of apostasy? Let us pray that Almighty God may so convict the men and women of the Church that we never come to that tragic spiritual condition.

NINEVEH NEVER RECOVERED

According to biblical historians, Nineveh never recovered from the destruction that God poured out upon it, and it became an example for all to see of how an angry God reacts when it comes to sin. The fate of Nineveh could well become the fate of all men and women who insist on continuing in sin and wickedness and rebellion against God and His Word.

Thank God that He's *"not willing that any should perish, but that all should come to repentance"* (2 Peter 3:9). We must run to Him quickly, so that we can maintain our relationship with Him and not be cut off.

When rebellion and disobedience push a merciful God to become jealous and to take vengeance on His adversaries, according to His prophet Nahum, no prayer or cries of repentance can change His decree. Though He is good, there is a limit to how much of man's rebellion God can allow:

> *The Lord is good, a strong hold in the day of trouble; and he knoweth them that trust in him. But with an overrunning flood he will make an utter end of the place thereof, and darkness shall pursue his enemies.*
> Nahum 1:7-8

According to biblical historians, Nineveh never recovered from the destruction that God poured out upon it, and it became an example for all to see!

God is more willing and ready to forgive us than we are to seek His forgiveness through repentance. Why is that? It's because He *"is love"* (1 John

4:16). And, in His love, He sends prophets to speak to us and show us our need.

We Need Modern Jeremiahs

In his time, Jeremiah, one of the major prophets in Israel, spoke many times to his people to reveal God's mind and purpose to the nation, to show them that God loved them with an everlasting love and that His covenant with them was an everlasting covenant. We need such prophets to speak to us today in America.

Will America ever prosper again? Will this nation rebound and regain the number one position—morally, economically and militarily in the world? To say yes would be encouraging, but in order for this to happen, America must become again the number one nation in the world in holiness, righteousness and truth. For America to receive again such blessings, this nation must be willing to repent, beginning with our churches. God has said:

> *Blessed is the nation whose God is the Lord; and the people whom he hath chosen for his own inheritance.*
>
> Psalm 33:12

The reverse of this statement is that the nation whose God is not the Lord will not be blessed. Instead, it will be cursed. This would mean that God was not on our side. This is a serious matter that calls for serious action on our part.

Every church must repent. Every professing Christian who believes that the Bible is the Word of God must repent. This repentance must begin with the smallest congregation in the poorest neighborhood, but it must continue all the way up to those in authority in the administration in Washington. No one can be excluded.

EVERY SOUL SHOULD BELIEVE AND OBEY

Here is one of the verses of the Bible that every soul should believe and obey:

If my people, which are called by my name, shall humble themselves, and pray, and seek my face, and turn from their wicked ways; then will I hear from heaven, and will forgive their sin, and heal their land.

2 Chronicles 7:14

The healing of the land here refers to the restoration and prosperity of everything that this nation depends on for its daily needs, from farming to its financial institutions. But until proper repentance comes, God will continue to send us wildfires, floods, the destruction of crops and forests and the pollution of our water supply.

Again, *"Judgment must begin at the house of God"* (1 Peter 4:17). This is the reason that all who call themselves Christians and understand the awesome power of God must begin, without reservation, to urgently seek His face to avert His wrath and receive His mercy. Every group of people who call themselves followers of the Lord Jesus Christ must now understand how loving God is and what He expects from us. We can have the mercy of God today, or we can rebel and face the untold misery of His wrath tomorrow.

GOD IS SEEKING US MORE THAN WE ARE SEEKING HIM

God is willing to forgive as men are willing to repent, but He always seems to be seeking men more than they are seeking Him:

> *Thus saith the LORD; Stand in the court of the LORD's house, and speak unto all the cities of Judah, which come to worship in the LORD's house, all the words that I command thee to speak unto them; diminish not a word: if so be they will hearken, and turn every man from his evil way, that I may repent me of the evil which I purpose to do unto them because of the evil of their doings.*
>
> Jeremiah 26:2-3

God is willing to forgive as men are willing to repent, but He always seems to be seeking men more than they are seeking Him!

In Jeremiah's day, God purposed to draw the attention of the people of Israel toward Him, and the only way, it seemed, that He could accomplish this was by allowing destruction to overcome them. Maybe then they would call upon Him, and if and when they did, He would deliver them from their troubles.

God is doing this very same thing today here in America and with many more of the rich nations around the world. When the root of our problems is sin, there can be no other solution but God's. Nothing that man can do on his own will reverse the destruction.

In recent years, we have witnessed (and even experienced) calamity after calamity. With television news now reaching into much of the world, such calamities are now seen in our living rooms, wherever they happen to occur. And yet, will man bow his knees and repent and call upon the Lord for mercy? Apparently not. Men believe that the nations somehow have the ability to chart their own course and to escape the consequences of the judgment and wrath of God, even as the calamities keep coming. Before a nation can recover from one disaster, a new one, greater than the last, is upon it.

WHO HAS THIS POWER?

Why are these disasters coming? Who has the power to send such things? The answer is one that many do not want to hear:

> *Shall a trumpet be blown in the city, and the people not be afraid? shall there be evil in a city, and the LORD hath not done it?*   Amos 3:6

Why is it that so many preachers are afraid to tell the truth when calamities occur? Are they, perhaps, afraid to appear unpatriotic, with no love for their country, if they tell the truth?

Through the centuries, when any prophet has spoken the truth, it showed that he loved his fellowman and wanted them to know what was happening so that they could bring themselves into line with God's goodness and blessings by repenting and then doing works of repentance. And when any preacher speaks the truth today, that has to be good for the nation.

But truth is not popular, and the popular preachers are often those who insist that there will be *"peace, peace,"* when, in reality, *"sudden destruction"* is on its way (1 Thessalonians 5:3).

INSTEAD OF REPENTING, MANY SEEM TO BECOME EVEN MORE WICKED

One of the amazing things about this generation is that men refuse to seek repentance and forgiveness. Instead, they increase their wickedness and corruption by committing even more abominations against our Holy God. Is God obligated to bless a nation that continues to turn its back to Him? His record reveals that He gives man space to repent, but when men refuse to hear His words and, instead, stand in total rebellion, then God acts in response with His divine justice and judgment.

God is so merciful and righteous that He will not punish us until we have purposed in our hearts to reject every means whereby He seeks to deliver us from our evil ways. God wants us to be blessed with all His goodness, peace and fellowship. He continually seeks ways and means to get our attention, sometimes with actions that we don't appreciate.

WITH GOD'S BLESSINGS COMES RESPONSIBILITY

Who can deny the fact that with God's blessings come responsibilities? This country received a powerful message on 9-11, and then God gave the nation ample time to come to Him in repentance and remorse. But, instead of coming to God and acknowledging their sins and the wickedness of pleasure and evil and immoral rebellion, men became even worse than the nations of Sodom and Gomorrah.

Next, God touched our most delicate treasure—the economy. His first touch was just a slap on the wrist, but when there was no positive response, He came the second time, and this time billions of dollars in assets disappeared overnight. The greed of men brought its inevitable harvest. Was this, perhaps, because of the sins of Sodom and Gomorrah?

When God judged those wicked cities, He called His actions *"good"* (Ezekiel 16:50). Not surprisingly, man rejects God's judgment and calls it evil. But we know that God is good, and the things He does are good as well. Man, in contrast, was born *"in sin"* and *"shapen in iniquity"* (Psalm 51:5), and his acts are sinful continually.

Our Failing Compassion

"Am I my brother's keeper?" (Genesis 4:9). This was the question Cain asked when he had slain his brother, but it is also a question that rich nations such as ours must ask themselves, when they look the other way as millions starve and die of hunger and malnutrition around the world. What does God have to say about this practice? What has He done historically to those who continually heaped up treasures for themselves and failed to give to the poor what God required of them?

Our recent financial meltdown is a direct result of the greed of mankind, but also of the judgment of God. In other words, God has taken away what man insisted on keeping for himself. Men looked on in amazement as billions of dollars suddenly vanished into nothingness. Only God could have done that, taking from man what he thought he could hide and keep for his tomorrows. God can take anything He wants from any man at any time, but man cannot reverse that process and take anything back from God. When will we learn?

Americans want to prosper and maintain the most powerful and wealthy nation on earth, but if this is to happen this country must be forgiven. All of the calamities we have suffered are a result of the judgment of the wrath of a holy God, and if we are to be forgiven and released from judgment, we must repent of our evil.

WATCHMAN,
WHAT OF THE NIGHT?

The Scriptures speak of a place called Dumah:

The burden of Dumah. He calleth to me out of Seir, Watchman, what of the night? Watchman, what of the night? The watchman said, The morning cometh, and also the night: if ye will inquire, inquire ye: return, come.

Isaiah 21:11-12

What is the watchman saying? The Living Bible says it this way:

Someone from among you keeps calling, calling to me: "Watchman, what of the night? Watchman, what of the night? How much time is left?" The watchman replies, "Your judgment day is dawning now. Turn again to God, so that I can give you better news. Seek for him, then come and ask again!"

> *Our recent financial meltdown is a direct result of the greed of mankind, but also of the judgment of God!*

What would happen if you were to ask your pastor this same question today: "Pastor, what of the night?"

By this, you would mean, How much time must we spend in this present darkness? And are we coming out of it? Or is this a night of utter darkness for which there will be no dawn?

Pastors are to be watchmen on behalf of their people, and they are to know how to seek the face of Almighty God and get answers for life's dilemmas. When asked, "Tell us what we must do to get an answer of hope from God," they should have an answer.

If America fails to repent, it will be as the nation that was asked, *"Watchman, what of the night? Watchman what of the night?"* And what will be the answer for America and the rest of the world? *"The morning cometh and also the night."* If America is to see another morning, then America must repent. And, as the prophet showed, if this nation fails to repent, our country will enter into a night for which there will be no morning:

> *Righeousness exalts a nation, but sin is a disgrace to any people.*   Proverbs 14:34, NIV

Right now this nation and the rest of the nations of the world are passing through a dark night. Will we see another morning? History records the fact that Dumah never saw a morning, for its people failed to repent.

WILL AMERICA RISE AGAIN?

Will America rise again? Will the nations of the world

arise from their trouble? Will we come out of this depression? Just as He did with Nineveh, the Lord has given America and the world a grace period. Now, it's up to us what we will do with it.

Comparing the nations today to the people of Nineveh, we see a common pattern. Wickedness increased until the nation became apostate. Why did they wait until there was no hope of turning back to God? Delayed repentance is nothing more than rebellion.

The fate of Nineveh will be the fate of America if we fail to repent, and it will be the fate of the rest of the world if it also fails to repent. God is the one and only Righteous Judge, and He knows the spiritual state of any nation, as no man knows it. The people of Sodom and Gomorrah didn't know, and they didn't care. The generation of Noah also didn't know. The righteous have nothing to worry about, but wicked and hypocritical Christians and those falsely confessing to be believers must repent now, while there is yet time.

America sowed and America must reap, and just like America, the whole world will reap in the same proportion as it has sown. Oh, Righteous Father, forgive us before it's too late. Beloved, let us concentrate on *Always Being Ready*.

CHAPTER 14

SEEK FORGIVENESS QUICKLY

Seek ye the LORD while he may be found, call ye upon him while he is near: let the wicked forsake his way, and the unrighteous man his thoughts: and let him return unto the LORD, and he will have mercy upon him; and to our God, for he will abundantly pardon.

Isaiah 55:6-7

Since we can never be sure about the timing of things, wisdom decrees that we always repent quickly, while

> *Lifted up further in pride, rather than immediately denounce this idea that he was some god, Herod took the opportunity to bask in the adulation of the crowd!*

there is still time. It is important to seek forgiveness quickly, while God's grace is being extended to us. Delaying repentance is a temptation that can result in irreversible and even eternal disaster. Comparing something that happened to Herod and the way he reacted to it and a similar thing that happened to Paul and the way he reacted will further demonstrate this important truth.

HEROD'S FOLLY

Herod, King over Judea in the time of Christ, was tempted to take the glory that belonged to Jehovah. He could have repented quickly, but he delayed, and it cost him his life and his soul:

And upon a set day Herod, arrayed in royal apparel, sat upon his throne, and made an oration unto them. And the people gave a shout, saying, It is the voice of a god, and not of a man. And immediately the angel of the Lord smote him,

*because he gave not God the glory: and he was eaten of
worms, and gave up the ghost.*　　　Acts 12:21-23

Herod was apparently a gifted speaker, and when
he had finished his *"oration"* that day, he was applaud-
ed by the crowd. That may be normal enough, but
what was not normal was that the people were saying
that he was a god and not a man. They may well have
been only trying to flatter this already proud man, but
he took their words very seriously. Lifted up further
in pride, rather than immediately denounce this idea
that he was some god, Herod took the opportunity to
bask in the adulation of the crowd.

SUCH PRAISE MUST BE OFFERED
TO GOD ALONE

But this was praise that should have been offered
only to God Himself. Would Herod be able to recognize that and ask the Lord for forgiveness? He clearly
could have, but he didn't. The temptation to enjoy the
praise of the crowd was just too much for him.

Then, without warning, sudden destruction hit
Herod. This king was *"eaten of worms"* and died. History records that his insides were eaten up. Wow!

What happened to Herod was a message from God
to everyone who witnessed it, heard about it or read
about it in the days to come. And it is a message to
every one of us. The man who refuses to repent will
be judged by the Ruler of the Earth.

WHAT SHOULD HEROD HAVE DONE?

What could Herod have done? For one, he could have rebuked the people for what they said (as Paul did in the book of Acts). He could have told the people that he was not a god, just a man (as Paul did). He could have gotten down from the high seat he was occupying, bowed himself to the earth and cried out to God for mercy for himself and the people who had erred in this serious way. He did none of these things. Instead, Herod enjoyed basking in the undeserved praise ... until it was too late.

Words like those spoken by this crowd must be rejected immediately. God is not willing that any should perish, but His grace also has limits. And, as we have discovered, when those limits are crossed only He knows for sure. If Herod had any inkling that what he was doing was wrong and that he should make it right, he failed to show it in time. His heart was not willing to surrender in that moment, and that was the only moment he had to do it.

He could have saved his life and saved his soul, but he didn't. He had already rejected the claims of the Gospel, and so there was no foundation upon which his heart could be humbled before the Almighty. In this way, his pride destroyed him.

THE DANGER OF GOING NOWHERE AND DOING NOTHING

Doing nothing can be a deadly act. In the chapter on forgiveness for departing from the will of God, I told the story of a man of God who was sitting under an oak tree doing nothing. It was in that very unguarded moment that temptation pursued him, and he was overcome by it. That very day his life came to an end, and his ministry was shipwrecked.

When David was tempted to sin with Bathsheba, he was on the rooftop of his house, walking around one evening. He was just going nowhere and doing nothing, and that fact got him into trouble:

> *And it came to pass in an eveningtide, that David arose from off his bed, and walked upon the roof of the king's house: and from the roof he saw a woman washing herself; and the woman was very beautiful to look upon.* 2 Samuel 11:2

Bathsheba was the wife of Uriah, but her illicit union with David produced a child. In response, David planned and executed the man's murder. Then the child died. All of this was the result of a man walking around one evening with nothing to do. It clearly doesn't pay.

IN CONTRAST TO HEROD, PAUL WAS SAVED

Paul saved his life through humility, rejecting the glory that belongs only to God (see Acts 14:8-18);

> *And when the people saw what Paul had done, they lifted up their voices, saying in the speech of Lycaonia, The gods are come down to us in the likeness of men.* Acts 14:11

Rather than bask, even for a few moments, in this illicit glory, Paul and Barnabas reacted quickly to defuse the dangerous situation and give all glory to whom it is due:

> *Which when the apostles, Barnabas and Paul, heard of, they rent their clothes, and ran in among the people, crying out, and saying, Sirs, why do ye these things? We also are men of like passions with you, and preach unto you that ye should turn from these vanities unto the living God, which made heaven, and earth, and the sea, and all things that are therein.* Acts 14:14-15

Herod had this same window of opportunity, but he did not have within himself the conviction of the Spirit or the remembrance of the Scriptures to teach him that God is not willing to share His glory with another. Every man who fails to give God glory suffers the consequences.

SEEKING FORGIVENESS FOR THE SINS OF OUR YOUTH

Our young people need to seek forgiveness from God because they are committing murder through abortion. Millions of innocent lives have now been snuffed out through this hideous crime. Those who have participated in this sin need to pray the prayer of David, seeking God's mercy and forgiveness:

> *Remember, O LORD, thy tender mercies and thy loving kindnesses; for they have been ever of old. Remember*

182

not the sins of my youth, nor my transgressions: according to thy mercy remember thou me for thy goodness' sake, O LORD.

Psalm 25:6-7

We know that no murderer can enter the Kingdom of Heaven, and there can be no doubt that abortion is murder. Every new life that is conceived in a woman's womb is a living soul, a person, just as God revealed in His Word:

> *Every man who fails to give God glory suffers the consequences!*

For thou hast possessed my reins: thou hast covered me in my mother's womb. I will praise thee; for I am fearfully and wonderfully made; marvellous are thy works; and that my soul knoweth right well. My substance was not hid from thee, when I was made in secret, and curiously wrought in the lowest parts of the earth. Thine eyes did see my substance, yet being unperfect; and in thy book all my members were written, which in continuance were fashioned, when as yet there was none of them.

Psalm 139:13-16

The problem is that doctors (who are not God) have been granted the right to determine what is right and what is wrong in this situation. But we cannot trust the philosophy of men when we are dealing with spiritual things, especially those principles of scripture that con-

183

cern our eternal destiny. Our salvation is too priceless to be entrusted to a man's interpretation of spiritual design.

All Must Repent

The doctors and nurses who participate in abortion procedures must repent. Mothers, young and old, who have aborted children must repent. The men involved, even young boys, must seek forgiveness with godly sorrow for committing such grotesque acts against the commandments of a Holy God.

In our public schools, young people are being told that they have done the right thing, but just at the wrong time. I am a witness to this fact. I personally heard it repeated several times to young girls in school assemblies, and consequently they came away from their counseling session thinking that they were not guilty of any serious wrongdoing. Since the Scriptures were taken out of our public schools, who can tell our young people that fornication and adultery are sins of immorality? They must be told, and they must be told that they need to repent for these sins. And, since the schools are not free to tell them, now only the Church remains to sow these truths into the hearts of our young people.

If a church is not properly taught, the people who attend it and even its leaders may consider that God must accept these young people as they are. They've done nothing wrong because "everybody's doing it." "So," the youth must reason, "if the teachers say I'm okay, the doctors say I'm okay, my parents say nothing, and my pastor also didn't say anything against my decision, why should

God be angry?" This is the reason we are admonished to preach the Word of God without fear or favor.

And the Ten Commandments are still part of that Word. They have not been changed in order to give men a license to sin. God forbid. Jesus didn't die so that mankind could live a life of debauchery. The shedding of His blood was *"for the remission of sins"* (Matthew 26:28) and the Holy Ghost came into the world to give us power to live free from the bondage of the devil.

Remember, therefore, what God has said:

Thou shalt not kill.   Exodus 20:13

Thou shalt not commit adultery.   Exodus 20:14

THE WORKS OF THE FLESH

The Scriptures enumerate in a very detailed way, *"the works of the flesh."* There are seventeen of them in the list, and it's clear how destructive they are, and yet they are all employed every single day through our popular media to further demonize modern mankind. It is literally impossible to walk our streets today and not see these things, and often we must repent just for the feeling of uncleanness we get passing them by in the street. Here are those *"works of the flesh"*:

Now the works of the flesh are manifest, which are these; adultery, fornication, uncleanness, lasciviousness, idolatry, witchcraft, hatred, variance, emulations, wrath, strife, seditions, heresies, envyings, murders, drunkenness, revellings, and such like: of the which I tell you before, as I have also told you in time past, that they which do such things shall not inherit the kingdom of God.

Galatians 5:19-21

There is power available to the child of God, through the Holy Spirit, to destroy all the works of darkness, so we must *"put on the whole armour of God"* (Ephesians 6:11). There is also cleansing for all who are willing to surrender their lives to Christ.

Here's a similar list from Paul's first letter to the Corinthians:

Know ye not that the unrighteous shall not inherit the kingdom of God? Be not deceived: neither fornicators, nor idolators, nor adulterers, nor effeminate, nor abusers of themselves with mankind, nor thieves, nor covetous, nor drunkards, nor revilers, nor extortioners, shall inherit the kingdom of God. And such were some of you: but ye are washed,

> ***There is power available to the child of God, through the Holy Spirit, to destroy all the works of darkness, so we must "put on the whole armour of God"!***

186

but ye are sanctified, but ye are justified in the name of the Lord Jesus, and by the Spirit of our God.

1 Corinthians: 6:9-11

The Lord reminds us that we were all wicked before we were delivered, so we cannot judge those whom we see every day doing all these evils. That's what we were like in the past. Now, however, we are called by the Lord to live in a completely different state of mind, and to know that anyone who is still outside the Church can be saved, just as we were, for God is *"no respecter of persons"* (Acts 10:34).

GOD'S DIVINE AND UNPREDICTABLE TIMING

Why repent quickly? Why seek forgiveness quickly? It is impossible to know the timing of the Rapture, or the time when Jesus will return to deliver the righteous from this world. That date is known only to the Father.

As we have noted, God is unpredictable when it comes to many things, and the day and hour of the Rapture is one of those unpredictables. It will come *"when ye least expect it,"* and Jesus said that no man knows the day nor the hour:

But of that day and hour knoweth no man, no, not the angels of heaven, but my Father only.

Matthew 24:36

Since the Rapture may come any day now, it is imperative that Christians maintain their spiritual position and not allow the enemy to turn them aside. Beloved, let us concentrate on *Always Being Ready.*

CHAPTER 15

A MESSAGE TO SINNERS AND BACKSLIDERS

Repent ye: for the kingdom of heaven is at hand.
                                        Matthew 3:2

Although this book has been written primarily for believers, there is an important message for every sinful man and woman alive today. It is found in the words of Jesus. He said, *"Repent ye: for the kingdom of heaven is at hand."* This was one of the most important and most consistent parts of His message when He was here on the earth.

Why does Jesus require that you repent? Believe me, it is not so that you can feel bad about yourself. Just the opposite is true. Through repentance, you can find God's forgiveness and have your life changed forever.

Please don't be deceived by the modernday Gospel that teaches salvation without repentance and forgiveness without confession of your sins. It won't happen. It never has been true, and it never will be true. Believe and obey the words of Jesus, and you will be saved and guaranteed a place at His side throughout eternity.

There is also an important message for every backslider on the face of this earth: Return to the Lord and seek to restore your relationship with Christ, that you might be found like the five wise virgins. They refused to allow their lamps to run out of oil as they awaited the coming of the bridegroom (see Matthew 25:1-8). Jesus likened their dedicated watchfulness to our necessary state as we await His return. Don't let the Bridegroom come and find your soul in a state of spiritual rebellion.

A Most Important Question

Now, dear reader, I must take this opportunity to ask you a most important question: Is your name written in the Book of Life? If so, you will be eligible to rise with our Lord in the Rapture with all His saints. Only those elect will escape the wrath to come:

And at that time shall Michael stand up, the great prince which standeth for the children of thy people: and there shall be a time of trouble, such as never was since there was a nation even to that same time: and at that time thy people shall be delivered, every one that shall be found written in the book.

Daniel 12:1

Wise men and women will be ready to rise to meet the Lord on that day. Those who have been foolish and found no time to repent and seek forgiveness will be left behind on this earth, to face the worst times of trouble the world has ever seen in all its sordid history. Please don't be offended by these truths. Accept the Savior today and secure your place in the eternal Paradise prepared for you by the Lord.

WHAT WILL YOUR END BE?

What will your end be?

And many of them that sleep in the dust of the earth shall awake, some

> *Those who have been foolish and found no time to repent and seek forgiveness will be left behind on this earth, to face the worst times of trouble!*

to everlasting life, and some to shame and everlasting contempt. And they that be wise shall shine as the brightness of the firmament, and they that turn many to righteousness as the stars for ever and ever.

Daniel 12:2-3

All that is needed to be included in those destined to *"awake to everlasting life"* and then *"to shine as the stars forever and ever"* is, first, to become a child of God through justification by faith in Christ, as a result of the work He accomplished on the cross. This should be followed by God's Gift of the Holy Spirit to empower you to live a victorious, holy Christian life. Then, do as the Scriptures admonish:

Watch ye therefore, and pray always, that ye may be accounted worthy to escape all these things that shall come to pass, and to stand before the Son of man.

Luke 21:36

Being prepared for the coming of the Lord means living in a state of relationship with Him, and that should be your motivation, rather than responding in fear to an end-time message. Beloved, let us concentrate on *Always Being Ready.*

Amen!

Just as a man can prevent trouble from thieves by keeping watch for them, so you can avoid trouble by ALWAYS BEING READY for my unannounced return. Matthew 24:43-44, TLB
(Emphasis Mine)

Ministry Page

Readers may contact the author at the following addresses:

Daniel Roberts
Omega Outreach Ministries, Inc.
145–95 222nd Street
Springfield Gardens, NY 11413

e-mail: danielroberts3@verizon.net
on the Internet: www.omegaoutreachministries.com